JESUS
The Master Teacher

JEANIE SHAW

Jesus The Master Teacher: Transforming Our Hearts

© 2024 by Jeanie Shaw

All rights are reserved. No part of this book may be duplicated, copied, translated, reproduced, or stored mechanically, digitally, or electronically without specific, written permission of the author and publisher. Printed in the United States of America.

ISBN: 978-1-958723-32-6.

All Scripture quotations, unless indicated, are taken from the Holy Bible, New International Version (NIV), ©2011 by Biblica, Inc. Used by permission. All rights reserved worldwide.

Cover design by Roy Appalsamy and interior layout by Toney Mulhollan. The text face is set in Minion Pro and Arial Narrow.

About the author: **Jeanie Shaw** is a teacher and communicator of spiritual growth. She received her Master's in Christian Spirituality and Formation from Regent University and her Doctorate in Spiritual Formation and Discipleship from Nazarene Theological Seminary. She serves as a Christian life coach, teacher, and spiritual director. She finds great joy in journeying alongside others, helping them discover God's presence as they navigate life's joys and challenges. Jeanie recently retired after serving for over four decades in full-time ministry, alongside her late husband. She considers her work with the underserved, particularly with orphans in Eastern Europe, a deeply formative part of her life. She resides in New England, enjoying close proximity to her four adult children and eight grandchildren, whom she adores. You can learn more about her ministry at riverfrontcoaching.com.

Theatron Press is an imprint of
Illumination Publishers International
www.ipibooks.com

CONTENTS

To Sam Laing, who taught with depth, understanding, and passion. His excitement in exploring the treasures in God's Word was as evident to me as an eager, young campus student as it was to his beloved Sunday school class with the elderly, where the Old Testament brought him and his students a richer understanding and experience of God. He loved to teach the Bible because he loved the author.
That love was contagious.

And to the memory of Richard Whitehead, my dad, aka "the walking concordance," whose zeal for God and the Bible overflowed whenever he taught.
I am forever grateful.

Introduction

Jesus the Master Teacher

Sweat poured from Jesus' brow as he walked in the heat of the day. As he stopped to remove a pebble from his sandal, he glanced at the group traveling with him, noting their weariness…and feeling his. He remembered a grouping of fig trees within a thirty-minute walk that could provide shade, and promised his followers he hadn't cursed those. There the group could take refreshment, and perhaps he would teach. A trained rabbi and one who could be considered a philosopher, Jesus was different from other teachers. He not only "talked the talk," but unlike anyone else, he walked the walk of perfect grace and truth.

I try to imagine walking with Jesus from place to place, listening to his teaching along the way. I like to think I would hang on his every word, eager to hear what he would say next, but would I? Do I?

I envision being dumbfounded by the love emanating from the core of his being. There could be no denying that Jesus' love for people implored him to teach. I would hope to closely observe his responses to people's pain and learn from the ways he compassionately taught and interacted with them. I believe the security he knew in his identity would make me feel secure, and I imagine being enthralled by the confidence with which he taught from that surety. After all, he knew God, he was God's beloved Son, and he *was* God—one with him in a way beyond human understanding.

As one who was with God from the beginning, he would be urgent to communicate the very heart of God. His words might startle me as I watch him teach with assurance while healing the sick and caring for the hurting, thus backing up his teaching. As I continue to watch him interact, I cannot help but notice the ways he demonstrates hospitality, particularly to the marginalized.

What motivates him to get his hands dirty, serving again and again? Why does he keep teaching? Watching this miracle worker, Master Teacher, King of kings, and Lord of lords stoop down as a humble servant would surely shock me.

As I followed Jesus even farther down the road, I would discover that he has long been devoted to learning, as evidenced by his quoting the Torah and bringing to light its connections to him as the Messiah. I would wonder how he exhibits such impeccable timing with his words and deeds. Somehow, he would know when the timing was right to address something, and when it wasn't. Would I be struck by the ways Jesus taught with the end in mind, explaining the big-picture biblical narrative and asking the big, important questions, or would I even notice? I would like to think I would be mesmerized by his questions, reflecting on their significance and realizing the answers were often found within the questions.

I would likely find myself confused, inspired, convicted, and comforted through stories Jesus told, and I think I would not be able to get them out of my head or heart as I lay in bed at night. As he continued to teach, perhaps I would notice that sometimes he stands and other times he sits. As he sits, I would find that I feel invited, along with others, to come close. I would be shocked by the ways his open facial expressions encourage people to sit near him, because I would never have seen this kind of inclusive invitation by someone so important.

As he teaches, I think I would wonder if he has X-ray vision, seeing directly into people's hearts. I mean, he *really* sees them, listening to their words and even the thoughts behind their words. How does he do this? I would marvel as I hear the words that flow from his lips as he speaks with the uncanny, irresistible combination of grace and truth. It would seemingly become obvious, if I watched and learned, that this Master Teacher is divine, but oh, so human as well. He even needs to rest, but remarkably knows when to rest and when to work. I would hear that he was once found napping on a boat in the middle of a storm. At other times, he would be known to wander off alone to be with his Father. "Every day he was teaching in the temple, and at night he would go out and spend the night on the Mount of Olives, as it was called" (Luke 21:37 NRSV).

The ability and privilege to physically journey beside Jesus would be gone too soon. His teaching had such a profound impact that after three years, it would cost him his life. What would his followers do now? Thankfully, I would learn that he walked again with some friends on a road to Emmaus, as he had risen from the dead! And finally, I would see him pass on this call to teach, trusting his disciples to take his message of redemption and this new kind of heavenly kingdom to all the world. I would likely be confused, but inspired and comforted by his promise that he would make his home with me in the form of his Spirit, which would continue to comfort, teach, and form me.

It is this Jesus, the Master Teacher, in whom I find meaning and purpose for life. As I follow this Master Teacher, I discover that his teaching, his life, and his presence allow my life and teaching to have meaning, to come alive, and to affect and infect (in the healthiest ways) those whose lives I touch. So, join me. Let's watch, listen, and learn as Jesus, the Master Teacher, teaches.

As we journey through several qualities of Jesus, the Master Teacher, in the following chapters, my goal is to allow these attributes to more deeply enter not just our minds, but also our hearts, transforming us more closely into the image of Christ, whom we were created to reflect. I intend to explore meanings behind the words he speaks, perhaps taking deeper peeks into his heart. I hope that through this look into Jesus' teachings, those of us who are teachers can become more Christ-like in our teaching and interactions, as we seek to align our hearts with his. But mostly, I pray we all stand in awe of our Master Teacher, "in whom are hidden all the treasures of wisdom and knowledge" (Colossians 2:3 ESV).

While thinking about several of Jesus' qualities as the Master Teacher, I asked my Facebook friends to share about teachers who had most impacted them, accompanied by reasons why. I will share several of their many meaningful responses, using them as quotes at the beginning of each chapter of this book. Not surprisingly, the good qualities they share fall in line with many of the ways Jesus taught.

Hopefully, you will continue this study of Jesus, the Master Teacher, beyond these few pages, as you keep growing and learning. I pray that by surveying even these few qualities I explore, we will become more eager and effective students and teachers. Because I believe that reflection is crucial for learning and teaching, throughout each chapter, I offer opportunities to "Pause to Consider," making space for reflective exercises designed to help apply these Jesus-qualities to our lives.

We are all students and teachers in some form or another. Some of you reading this book teach professionally in secular settings, while others regularly teach the Bible or want to learn to do so more effectively. We also teach as we parent, coach, or function in our jobs. All relationships include some form of teaching, through things we say and don't say. Good teaching also demands a whole lot of continual learning. We never outgrow the need to be taught, no matter how experienced we are. Whatever form your teaching takes, Jesus' example makes us better people, and better teachers. His teaching styles are not meant to simply enhance our teaching, adding spice and nuance, but to transform our hearts so that the things we learn from him and subsequently pass on to others reflect his heart and encourage an intimate relationship with him. Please spend time with these reflections individually or in a discussion group. Pause to consider. They are designed to help us grow as learners, teachers, parents, friends, coaches, neighbors, and in any and every relational connection.

I pray that as we reflect on Jesus, the Master Teacher, and subsequently reflect on our own hearts, we discover increased intimacy with him that reaches from deep inside our hearts, overflowing into the lives of those we touch as we learn and teach. With this challenge in mind, my prayer as I began each chapter was this:

Bless these pages, O Lord.
May they receive words
that bring humility, understanding
and wisdom
from one taught by Jesus,
the Master Teacher.
Open my eyes and ears to learn and discern
so that my heart is filled with you
as I point others to you,
the Master Teacher.

My favorite teachers were those who invited questions and comments; who never belittled "wrong" answers. I found the safe space to sort of think out loud. This helped me to learn more by recognizing the weaknesses in my answers, understanding other factors and points of view, and developing better critical thinking skills. – Ann

The teacher's enthusiasm for the content made it favorable to remember the material. – Mary

What I remember is how they made me feel…their enthusiasm for the subject they taught, and the way they conducted the class. Teachers who love what they're teaching and welcome questions and discussion have by far made the biggest impact on me. – Sarah

My best teachers were those who excelled at sparking curiosity…those who helped us formulate/verbalize questions. – Summer

The ones I remember the most are those who truly loved and were passionate about their subject. I learned the most from them because they did whatever they could to get me excited to learn. – Karen

My best teacher empowered rather than victimized me, instilling that I was a decision away from achieving great goals. The teacher taught that each generation could lift the next onto their shoulders, with the hope they will outsee and outgrow those who have gone before. The teacher prepared us to discover new things we could not imagine ourselves, rather than forcing us to "color inside the lines" or instilling fear of stepping outside time-honored traditions. The teacher was aware and taught us this would only bring stagnation to the individual, the field of study, and ultimately all of humanity. John taught that even Jesus taught his disciples that they would see and do greater things than he did, and Paul echoed the same sentiment in his letters. The best teachers give others freedom to grow and outgrow them. It is no wonder that when we are the recipient of such love, it is an overwhelming and compelling experience. – Spence

Maybe the greatest teachers are just those who love us the most. – Gillian

Chapter One

The Master Teacher and Motivation

He had nowhere to lay his head or a place to call home, yet spoke of a home that would fill all longings—a place where we could belong. Though people clamored to listen as he taught, his closest disciples often missed his points, messing up continually. At times, his teaching was well received, and in other instances, it was confronted and opposed, even violently. Many flinched at his words but, enthralled, kept coming to hear more. His life gave substance to his words, but he was often misunderstood. Yet somehow, day after day, Jesus found motivation to teach. He taught until his last breath.

Since Jesus faced so many obstacles, what caused him to keep on teaching? It was certainly not the accolades or the paycheck. Did he feel obligated? Did fear move him? Did he teach to find acceptance or to find his identity? Did he wish for recognition? I pose these questions because too often these thoughts motivate us as humans. What made Jesus keep on teaching when there was seemingly nothing in it for him? This is the question we will explore.

Pause to Consider:

- What most often motivates me? Obligation? Recognition or desire for acceptance? To gain some sense of worth? Compassion? Faith?

Our motivation to teach (or learn) can ebb and flow, is sometimes fleeting, and is often illusive. Recently, one of my coaching clients, a young minister, expressed difficulty separating his desire to do well at his job (which understandably includes teaching others about Jesus) from a heartfelt motivation. We can all struggle with motivation. He shared that though he loves God and people, his teaching too often felt dutiful, and he struggled with thoughts that his success as a minister was overly dependent on him and his teaching ability. This caused angst, robbing him of the joy he desired and causing him to question his calling.

As he spoke, I remembered times past when I have plugged along dutifully. While duty and obedience are sometimes underrated, I believe Jesus came to bring life to the full (John 10:10). I also believe his promise that learning from his teaching brings rest to our souls (Matthew 11:28–30). However, when my motivation gets off track, teaching in any form becomes self-reliant and often burdensome. "Life to the full" can become "life full of self-dependance," and "rest for the soul" can become hijacked by "restlessness about what others think of me." During such times, regrettably, when motivation goes awry, people can become "someone to teach" more than someone to know and love who was made in God's image and whom God dearly loves. If this happens, our teaching can become rote, dutiful, or an exercise in rhetoric rather than being inwardly motivated by the love of Christ and love for people. I pray to see every person as a treasure created in the image of God, whom I can simply love before, during, and following any teaching opportunity.

As Jesus continues to transform me, I gain deeper joy and desire to teach out of love. Just love. I pray to have the humility to eagerly see, hear, and learn from everyone…to value them and respect them. Every person, without exception, was created in the image of God and is meant to reflect that image, having something valuable to offer. Everyone is worthy of respect. After I shared with my client about further ways to learn from Jesus' motivation as the Master Teacher, he shared with me his wise journal entry concerning motivation:

> **Question:** Is the opposite of control, love? When I focus on truly loving others, it's less about the "how" of them becoming Christians. A focus on love takes the mind off the process and puts it more on the person and on Jesus. You see that Jesus can change them and their life. Control focuses on all the steps required. Control focuses on me and my abilities. Control focuses on how I say things and thus can make love feel ungenuine and part of a process. Control puts conversion on me; love leaves conversion with God. Love always trusts…trusts that it's in God's hands. Love really does

take your mind deeply off the process and bring into heart Jesus' words, "Love your neighbor as yourself."

He told me how different, how much better he felt by changing his mindset, though he mentioned it was not easy to do or to maintain.

When we can view a person as one made in God's image and bestowed with a soul of infinite value and dignity, we will begin to see them as Jesus does. After all, Jesus was willing to become human and die for them, so they deserve to be greeted and beheld with respect and appreciation. When we remain keenly aware that every person has a God-given soul, we will look for that transcendent, eternal spark within and know they are just like us, in need of Jesus' redemption that lights that spark.

Pause to Consider:

- Do you think there is an antithesis between love and control? If so, why?
- If not, what is the reason or motivation behind a desire to control?
- How does the desire to control show up or sneak up in your life? What does control have to do with motivation?
- How might you grow in seeing each person as a treasure, beloved by God, made in his image?

Edward Deci and Richard Flaste, in their book, *Why Do I*

Do What I Do? Understanding Self-Motivation, report on their studies about motivation. Noting our competitive culture, they learned that people who were rewarded for sales displayed less subsequent intrinsic motivation than those who had simply been asked to do their best. The experience of competing had undermined their inner motivation.[1] They learned that motivating people is not something that gets done to them but rather something they do.

Pause to Consider:

- Has competition at times undermined your motivation? If so, what were the circumstances and how did you change that?
- What do you think the authors mean about motivating people being not something that gets done to you, but rather something you do?

Motivation of Love through Choosing

The authors' findings resonate with Jesus' teachings: "Love the Lord your God with all your heart and with all your soul and with all your mind and with all your strength. The second is this: 'Love your neighbor as yourself.' There is no commandment greater than these" (Mark 12:30–31). Obedience to the greatest commandment comes from within. As Jesus teaches

---

[1] Edward L. Deci and Richard Flaste, *Why We Do What We Do: Understanding Self-Motivation* (London: Penguin Books, 1996), 33.

here, it comes from a heart motivated by love rather than an expectation to be measured. The authors continue:

> It is forever being said that people need to be controlled more, that they need to be told what to do and held accountable for doing it. But nothing in the experiments has given credence to that view as the typical condition of life. Of course, limit setting is important, but an overemphasis on control and discipline seems to be off the mark. It represents a demeaning depiction of human experience, and its primary function may just be to provide certain people with an easy rationalization for exerting power over others.
>
> Providing choice, in the broad sense of that term, is a central feature in supporting a person's autonomy. It is thus important that people in positions of authority begin to consider how to provide more choice....
>
> The main thing about meaningful choice is that it engenders willingness. It encourages people to fully endorse what they are doing; it pulls them into the activity and allows them to feel a greater sense of volition; it decreases their alienation. When you provide people choice, it leaves them feeling as if you are responsive to them as individuals. And providing choice may very well lead to better, or more workable, solutions than

ones that would have been imposed.[2]

Some people, particularly those struggling to overcome addictive behaviors, may need to choose a high-accountability relationship to help them overcome bad habits or even sins. But key to their success is their choice to receive such help. Teaching carries with it a sense of authority, and while Jesus, the Son of God, possessed all authority, even Jesus left people with choice. He offered a new way of thinking and living yet offered autonomy to those he taught. Certainly their responses had ramifications, but as the Master Teacher, Jesus reached beyond their actions into their hearts. Through his teaching, he built an alliance with his disciples as they joined him in his mission. As he stayed with them longer as their Master Teacher, he no longer called them servants but friends (John 15:15). Friends work together as fellow workers, and followers of Jesus are God's fellow workers (1 Corinthians 3:9 ESV).

Motivation that willingly joins God in his work rather than asking God to join us in ours comes from a different place. It is tempting to motivate others by asking them to join our mission. A moving and inspiring song, a favorite in my church, is entitled "Men Who Dream." The lyrics express a passion for seeing souls saved. We enthusiastically sing the words, "We have a God who shares our dreams." I get the meaning, but how I wish it were phrased differently to instead express "We serve a God

---

[2] Deci and Flaste, *Why We Do*, 34.

whose dreams we share." I don't wish to bash this wonderful song, as it is also one of my favorites. I just want to reflect on the vast difference between joining God in his dreams and asking him to join ours. Do you see the difference? The first subtly takes over control. Motivation built on God's dreams becoming ours is so much deeper and more sustainable than asking God to join ours.

Pause to Consider:

- What is the difference in meaning between these two phrases, "We have a God who shares our dreams" and "We serve a God whose dreams we share?"
- What does it mean to you to be motivated by joining God in his dreams instead of asking him to join yours?

What motivated Jesus, and how did he motivate those he taught? As we will see in a later chapter, his teaching often asked questions that brought his hearers choices. "Do you want to be made well?" (John 5:6 NRSV). "Do you want to leave too?" (John 6:67 ERV). Jesus also included his students/disciples in decisions, such as how to feed a crowd of 5,000-plus hungry listeners (Matthew 14:13–21). While he instructed them to give the people something to eat, he also called them to think beyond what was physically possible and turn to faith. His "lesson" was not about cooking or even hospitality, but instead reached toward the deeper motivations of compassion, faith, and trust. He taught them that faith combined with what they had was enough. Faith and trust would become motivating factors for his disciples and must become motivating factors for us. He taught them to have compassion for people rather than sending them away. This was also a motivating factor for Jesus' teaching and would become motivation for his disciples…eventually. Compassion was at the very heart of Jesus' motivation.

"As he went ashore, he saw a great crowd; and he had compassion for them, because they were like sheep without a shepherd; and he began to teach them many things" (Mark 6:34 NRSV).

The Desire to Serve Motivates

Jesus' motivation to teach came also from his desire to serve. He did not come to earth to become a servant; he came because he already was a servant. Service was intrinsic within him. For God so loved he gave (John 3:16). Jesus states this intent in Mt 20:28: "Just as the Son of Man did not come to be served, but to serve, and to give his life as a ransom for many." His servant heart motivated him to teach again and again, whether when feeding a hungry crowd, gathering the children in his arms to bless them, or healing his friend's mother-in-law. He kept on serving while teaching, because he came as a servant.

Just as a parent wakes up in the night to comfort a scared or hungry child, or a caregiver sacrifices their freedom to tend to a loved one, or a neighbor cares for an immigrant, or someone sacrifices their comfort for the needs of another (be it a need for time, attention, or money), or a donor gives a kidney to a dying friend, the desire to serve comes from a place of love deep inside. Jesus even served his enemies; he could not do otherwise. He was motivated because his love caused him to serve. He served without favoritism, washing the feet of Judas as tenderly as all the others.

When service is not motivated from within, people's needs will embitter us, annoy us, or bring out an entitlement born of pride rather than being willing to serve. In John 4, as Jesus taught a Samaritan woman at the well, it seems significant that the scripture includes the statement, "But no one asked, 'What do you want' or 'Why are you talking to her?'" (John 4:27). These kinds of questions would have been born from self-focus, as if they thought his motivation for teaching her was about his needs, rather than his desire to serve her through his teaching. But no one asked these questions. Perhaps Jesus' servant heart was so well known that these questions did not need to be asked. His followers may have realized that something significant was happening in this conversation. At times, the lines can blur when our teaching comes from a focus on self rather than the purest concern for the life of another. Jesus' teaching stemmed from the latter. Always.

Pause to Consider:

- Why do you think the scripture in John 4 includes the phrase, "No one asked, 'What do you want?'"
- Do you ever find yourself seeking something personal when you teach? When can teaching become more

about you than the ones you teach?

- Reflect on a time when you were motivated to serve first and then teach versus teaching before or without thinking much about serving. Why might serving or not serving be significant in how you teach?

Love Motivates

The Father, Son, and Spirit created humankind for relationship. God (the three in one) longed to dwell and walk with us from the beginning. From the introduction of sin and beyond, that very good creation became flawed, digressing as hearts turned from God toward other gods, self-direction, and self-will. Yet God, Jesus, and the Spirit desired to redeem creation and restore the relationship, offering a different kind of kingdom that envisioned on earth what is in heaven, where moth and rust cannot destroy (Matthew 6:20) and which is unshakable (Hebrews 12:28). This is what Jesus taught us to pray. "Your kingdom come, your will be done, on earth as it is in heaven" (Matthew 6:10). Such is his desire to redeem, restore, and renew us all as his people, along with all of creation. His kingdom on earth as it is in heaven.

Every people group, prophet, and finally Jesus, who was God incarnate, was involved in orchestrating the plan for God's will to be done on earth as it is in heaven. This plan was for God to be with us, dwelling in us—a redeemed creation. Jesus longs for our relationship with him and with each other; this is what motivated him to come to earth, live, and die. His desire for a relationship of love was taught with repetition as Jewish households quoted the Shema prayer daily (Deuteronomy 6:4–9), and this prayer still serves as the greatest commandment.

> "Teacher, which is the greatest commandment in the Law?"
>
> Jesus replied: "'Love the Lord your God with all your heart and with all your soul and with all your mind.' This is the first and greatest commandment. And the second is like it: 'Love your neighbor as yourself.' All the Law and the Prophets hang on these two commandments." (Matthew 22:36–40)

Jesus' famous teaching on the hillside, which we know as the Sermon on the Mount, encapsulates his teaching about this new "kingdom of heaven" way to live, turning the thinking of this world on its head. It is this unshakable kingdom that Jesus longs for his followers to know. After all, he knew what it was like, as this was the kingdom he left to come to earth and allow us to be citizens of a new kingdom.

I have never been more aware than of late of the brokenness of the world in which we live. Anger, hatred, discord, immorality, entitlement, injustice, bitterness, and all sorts of conflicts and a desire to dominate fill our world, governments, schools, workplaces, and homes, and even too many of our churches. Jesus knew that the kingdom of heaven on earth (and the accompanying upside-down teaching of how to be citizens of this kingdom) is the only alternative to chaos and the downward spiral of deception leading to death. What a motivating thought to realize that nothing in politics, schools, or even sometimes the kingdom-of-earth ways we are tempted to function as churches can change the world; but Jesus' redemptive love can. Little by little, the kingdom "on earth as it is in heaven" can bring healing, justice, virtue, compassion, forgiveness, peace, and joy. What a motivating thought. What a concept to learn and teach.

Pause to Consider:

- Reflect on what it might look like to see God's redeemed kingdom on earth. How does (or does not) the understanding of God's kingdom on earth motivate you to live? Motivate you to teach?
- The Jews taught and quoted the Shema prayer daily. How might you incorporate a daily reminder of your ultimate motivation?
- Read the Sermon on the Mount in Matthew 5–7. Does this way of life motivate and infiltrate your teaching?
- For parents, how might you teach and motivate your children with these kingdom values?

Ultimately, Jesus' teaching was motivated by love. Jesus understood that people were caught in the lies of the evil one, who can never deliver what he promises. When Jesus saw people enslaved by sin, injustice, and pain, he longed to free them. Though all were not physically freed or healed, his teaching offered freedom from bitterness, loneliness, lostness, and finally death. His teaching reached through pain, desiring to take it away but always willing to be with us in ours. He became acquainted with grief. God has always cared for the oppressed, and Jesus, the exact representation of God (Hebrews 1:3), demonstrates God's love. Ever since sin entered the world, oppression, sickness, and captivity have reigned. God's *hesed* (steadfast love), expressed through Jesus, came to free the captives and tend to the poor, sick, and oppressed. His teaching ministry began with this intent, this motivation, as seen in Luke 4:

> He went to Nazareth, where he had been brought up, and on the Sabbath day he went into the synagogue, as was his custom. He stood up to read, and the scroll of the prophet Isaiah was handed to him. Unrolling it, he found the place where it is written:
>
> "The Spirit of the Lord is on me,
> because he has anointed me
> to proclaim good news to the poor.
> He has sent me to proclaim freedom for the prisoners
> and recovery of sight for the blind,
> to set the oppressed free,
> to proclaim the year of the Lord's favor."
> Then he rolled up the scroll, gave it back to the at-

> tendant and sat down. The eyes of everyone in the synagogue were fastened on him. He began by saying to them, "Today this scripture is fulfilled in your hearing." (Luke 4:16–21)

Thus began Jesus' ministry of compassion and healing. Matthew 4:23 tells us Jesus went through Galilee, teaching in the synagogues, proclaiming the good news of the kingdom, and curing every disease and sickness among the people. Jesus' teaching was also motivated by people's needs and pain. In John 11, Jesus, moved by the pain of grief (his own and Mary's and Martha's) after the death of Lazarus, then taught on the resurrected life. He would offer an opportunity for a new way to live and a hope for eternal life. Throughout the Gospels, we find Jesus' compassion preceding his teaching. We see him moved by a sinful woman's extraordinary act of love and gratitude (Luke7:36–50). He knew her rejection and shame, and he showed her love as he taught. We can note that in this same account, Jesus also loved Simon the Pharisee, who needed a heart change from judgment to mercy. Moved by their individual circumstances, he taught Simon and the sinful woman each according to their need. Whether he taught groups of leaders and teachers, or whether he taught one impoverished individual, Jesus' love and compassion moved him to meet their needs. People's needs motivated him—as long as people had needs, he would respond. He could not do otherwise.

Pause to Consider:

- What is the difference between teaching from humility and teaching from a position of "better than?"
- How might you become more personally aware and motivated by the needs of the oppressed, poor, and marginalized?
- How might compassion and teaching go together?

Jesus taught audiences of one with as much zeal as when he taught crowds. The numbers didn't motivate him. The needs did. He was as easily motivated to teach a hurting "one" such as the Samaritan woman (John 4) as he was to teach the educated, "successful" many. He longed to gather even the prideful Pharisees and religious leaders who opposed him as a mother hen gathers her chicks (Matthew 23:37). He cried over the city of Jerusalem (Luke 19:41–44) when pained over their hardness of heart. His motivation to teach stemmed from his compassion for the people as he saw their situation. Jesus knew that his message of redemption and hope could change their lives forever. He knew his teachings held the power to transform the ways people interacted with each other, having huge ramifications for the poor, the captives, the handicapped, and the oppressed.

Mark 1:38–39 tells us that Jesus came to preach, and his words accompanied his compassion. It is such a simple concept, but we can become so familiar with the gospel message that it becomes less than the incredible, amazing, life-changing news it is. Jesus never lost site of the power of the good news he came to bring. This served to motivate him as he taught. Nothing we teach or preach is as powerful and life-giving as this gospel of Jesus.

When I try a new dish that gives my palette a party, celebrate accomplishments of my children or grandchildren, notice something of extraordinary beauty, cry because of a moving musical score, find a bargain, or even watch a reel that makes me laugh, the first thing I want to do is share it with someone. Jesus taught the most incredible news ever known. He is that good news. Is it he who motivates you?

Pause to Consider:

- Consider a time when you were so full of gratitude for Jesus' love that you couldn't hold it in. What did that motivation feel like? What does it look like in your life when you fail to be motivated by the goodness Jesus offers?
- What are some ways you might become more aware of opportunities to let teaching flow from your love?

Companionship Motivates

Jesus, moved by compassion as he lived and taught, was not alone. He lived, moved, and taught in union with his Father and the Spirit. I find companionship to be a deeply motivating factor. When I know someone is with me, I can step beyond my comfort zone, knowing someone is there to catch me when I fall, can encourage me to move forward, or will just bear witness to my "being." Since the beginning of time, when the Spirit hovered over the waters as Jesus created, the Spirit was with Jesus. And God was with Jesus. At Jesus' baptism, John recounts the Spirit resting on Jesus as a dove (Matthew 3:16). He took many forms but was always with and in Jesus, as the Father, the Son, and the Spirit remain one.

Jesus describes the Spirit as our helper and comforter (*parakletos*) who guides, teaches, reminds, gives wisdom, tells us what to say, hears, interprets, speaks, and glorifies (see John 14–16). The Spirit was with him from the beginning, and the Spirit is still at work today, promised by Jesus to make his dwelling place with us. In fact, we have greater access to Jesus living in us through the Spirit than those did who walked with him physically. If I could insert a "mind blown" emoji, it would fit right here. God's Spirit lives in me. God experienced humanity so I could experience divinity.

"But the Advocate, the Holy Spirit, whom the Father will send in my name, will teach you everything, and remind you of all that I have said to you" (John 14:26 NRSV). We are not alone. The Spirit is at work in the lives of Christians, teaching, reminding, advocating, and motivating us in ways beyond human reasoning and book-smart teaching. This companionship offers me great incentive for living and teaching.

Such calling and divine empowerment motivate in a way that exceeds mere human motivation. Jeremiah described this phenomenon:

But if I say, 'I will not mention his word
    or speak anymore in his name,'
his word is in my heart like a fire,
    a fire shut up in my bones.
I am weary of holding it in;
    indeed, I cannot." (Jeremiah 20:9)

In Luke 19:37–40, Jesus fulfilled Old Testament prophecy as he rode into Jerusalem on a donkey while people praised God for all the miracles they had seen. The people, not understanding, still wanted him to be the physical king who would defeat Roman oppression. In response to this "triumphal entry," which was in contrast to worldly kings, who rode in on fine horses, the Pharisees told Jesus to rebuke those joyful disciples. Jesus replied, "If they keep quiet, the stones will cry out." Then as Jesus approached Jerusalem and saw the city, he wept over it and said, "If you, even you, had only known on this day what would bring you peace—but now it is hidden from your eyes" (Luke 19:42). The rocks would have greater understanding, belief, and motivation than the Pharisees and the rest of the populace. They had missed the motivating factor of love.

The coming of Jesus is such good news that even the rocks cry out and can't be contained. The Spirit within brings that motivating fire in the bones and sounds the clarion call. The Spirit was always with Jesus, and the Spirit can motivate and empower us as well.

Jesus never quit teaching. In his dying moments, he taught

forgiveness and compassion. He saw the needs of others and was motivated by love, because he is love. Because he loved, he offered people a choice. Without choice, people are robotic rather than motivated from within. Jesus was motivated to serve as he lived and taught, because he came to serve, not to be served. May we learn from Jesus, the Master Teacher, as we seek to join him in his mission, empowered by the Spirit who motivates and transforms us to be more and more like Jesus.

Pause to Consider:

- Is your connection with the Spirit such that your motivation often burns from within?
- Do you allow the Spirit to motivate and empower you, or do you tend toward working harder from your own willpower and strength?
- How do you actively rely on and engage the Spirit?
- Do you believe Jesus teaches you because he really loves you, or because he just teaches good teachings?

The teachers I learned most from were the ones who taught people. The ones I learned the least from were the ones who taught lessons. – Roger

My favorite teachers are the ones who are fair and equitable. They apply rules to all, not just the favored few, and they treat each student with respect. I admire those teachers who have a balance of pushing you to meet your potential and meeting the needs of individual students. – Ilona

I think of teachers who actually cared. Teachers who took note of my strengths, weaknesses, personality. – Kristen

He said what the Bible actually said rather than what I would like it to say. – Greg

My best teachers treated me with a curiosity of who I am, and not just an exchange of information. – Angie

They really made me feel they cared about my needs and helped me not only succeed in their class, but in life. They took time to check in with each of us and listen and talk, sometimes even changing the way a lesson was taught to help one or more of us meet our goals. – Elise

One of my favorite teachers noticed some of my hidden talents, when I felt invisible to most. I remember some of the specific things he said and taught, and cherish his perspective to this day. – Laura

Some of my favorite teachers were very creative with the curriculum, customizing it for our different learning styles. I'll never forget the teacher who made sure every student in our class had a prom date. – Peggy

They have clear knowledge of what they teach, but they don't act like they know everything. They convey what they teach in story form, not just conveying facts or information. They connect their material with the audience. They bring personal examples to what they teach. It's not just abstract or theoretical concepts. They can share their own strengths, weaknesses, and struggles in the process. They are not afraid to let others laugh at them. – Aaron

Chapter Two

The Master Teacher and Identity

Henri Nouwen, a Catholic priest and ivy league professor-turned-caregiver to a mentally challenged man, once gave a seventeen-minute sermon that touched me as much as any sermon ever has. He spoke about being "God's beloved," noting that we often seek to gain our identity through what we do, what we have, and what others think of us. He contrasts these thoughts with the ways we live life when we truly believe we are beloved by God. I don't mean simply believing the fact, but instead internalizing and experiencing this love. When a teacher, or anyone, fails to wrestle with and come to deep convictions concerning their God-given identity, their life and teaching will be compromised by their own presuppositions and unresolved views of God and self.

Pause to Consider:

- When you reflect on your sense of identity, what are ways your views of yourself are affected by what you have, what you do, and what others think of you?

Identity as God's Beloved

I like to imagine what Jesus might have felt when he descended into the Jordan River to be baptized by his cousin, John the Baptizer, and the Spirit of God rested on him while the voice of God radiated from heaven to earth with the words, "This is my beloved Son. Hear him" (Matthew 3:16–17 NKJV). I wonder what it would be like to hear God say I am his beloved. Beloved son. Beloved daughter. What an identity! Amazingly, this is meant to be our identity as sons and daughters of the Almighty God. This is who God says we are. As I read through the Scriptures, they are replete with God letting his creation know that they are loved and that he longs for relationship with them (us).

It's hard to fathom that we are created in his image, beloved by him. It is difficult to accept this identity in a world where what we do, what we have, and what others think of us tend to matter deeply. In my mind's eye, as I follow Jesus farther and listen to him teach, his confidence in his identity radiates as he takes off his outer garments, stoops down, and washes his disciples' feet.

> Jesus knew that the Father had put all things under his power, and that he had come from God and was returning to God; so he got up from the meal, took off his outer clothing, and wrapped a towel around his waist. After that, he poured water into a basin and began to wash his disciples' feet, drying them with the towel that was wrapped around him. (John 13:3–5)

Jesus knew all power was given to him, that he had come from God and was returning to God. This identity, and his knowledge and acceptance of it, allowed him to give fully and completely. He was not focused on "filling" his identity. As he taught, Jesus' focus was decidedly on those he taught. As he served, he never appeared to feel unworthy due to upbringing, culture, or education. He was not servile while serving others; he simply focused on loving people. And as he served, his teachings held powerful sway. He knew who he was, and it did not depend on what he had, his profession, or what others thought of him.

As I continue, in my imagination, to watch Jesus approach Judas and place a basin of water at his feet, I imagine Jesus looking at him while gently scrubbing his feet with the cool water, carefully removing layers of dust and grime. I envision him tenderly drying them before re-tying the sandals he had placed back on Judas's feet. There is no mention of rough treatment as he washes Judas. He washes Judas's feet just as he does everyone else's. How did Jesus have such surety of his identity that he could love someone who would betray him just as much as he loved the rest? His understanding of his identity allowed him to empty himself. Until we are sure of our identity, we will be so busy trying to fill ourselves that it becomes impossible to empty ourselves. Jesus knew who he was. Do we know who we are?

Knowing Where We Come From and Where We Are Going

As I continue to observe Jesus, I would likely feel troubled watching the Pharisees challenge him as he taught that he was the light of the world. His response would stop me in my tracks:

> Jesus answered, "Even if I testify on my own behalf, my testimony is valid, for I know where I came from and where I am going. But you have no idea where I come from or where I am going. You judge by human standards; I pass judgment on no one. But if I do judge, my decisions are true, because I am not alone. I stand with the Father, who sent me." (John 8:14–16)

"I know where I came from and where I am going." What profound knowledge. Knowing where we come from, whose we are, and where we are going changes everything. Jesus confidently continues because he knows his words are true. "You know me, and you know where I am from. I have not come on my own. But the one who sent me is true, and you do not know him" (John 7:28 NRSV). It seems from these two statements that, while people *should* know who he is and where he is from, they do not really understand. Thankfully, Jesus knows and understands.

Whether young or old, we tend to spend much time and effort seeking to gain our identity and acceptance from what we have, what we do, and what others think of us. We can be concerned with who and how many "like" our social media posts or whether our videos receive hits. Teachers can seek identity from responses to lessons or articles published or feel insecure as to whether their material is helpful, or whether they even have any "right" to teach. Our identities can be affected by what our colleagues think of us or how well we perform in school, sports, or jobs. It's exhausting to decipher the ways we view ourselves when convoluted by unhealthy identities.

Identity Starts with Our View of God

I believe the ways we view ourselves stem from our view of God. If we view God as punitive and unloving, it is hard to view ourselves (or others) as God's beloved. If we see God as disinterested and far away, we will leave out the most important aspect of Jesus' teaching: love. We will feel we can never measure up, or we may assume that no one really cares for us. This might also tempt us to teach with a judgmental posture. Because Jesus was so sure of his identity, he taught with authority, vulnerability, humility, and love. His actions and teachings were always for the benefit of others, as he already knew where he came from and where he was going.

Pause to Consider:

- Do I view God more as a punitive judge or a God of grace and mercy?
- How does either view affect my view of myself?
- How does this view affect the ways I respond to and teach others?

We often view things not as they are, but as we are. For

instance, someone who has been abused will often feel they are less than valuable. They may not have experienced intimacy that is safe. Someone who has been abandoned struggles with believing they are worth sticking around for. After all, someone didn't think they were. Others may have been neglected or experienced conditional love. Some have been constantly berated, with all their faults pointed out front and center. All these traumas affect one's sense of identity. The rational brain is incapable of talking the emotional body out of its own reality, so the body needs to experience a different reality firsthand.[3] Only when we accept our identity as God's beloved can we experience a reality that does not depend on the failings of those who have chipped away at the beautiful image of God in which we were created. This image is our truest identity. Our challenge becomes accepting and believing this. May the Spirit empower us to do so!

People damaged by trauma seek to assimilate what happened into their views of their identity, accommodating what happened to create new models and fundamental beliefs. They can think things happen to them because of what they deserve, and that God is never pleased with them. Or our identities become plagued with questions concerning what kind of God allows such-and-such to happen and what kind of person are we that these things happened to us, as if we deserve all bad things. Depending on how we process loss, abuse, and rejection, we can either become wiser, stronger, and more compassionate or stuck, angry, controlling, and scared. These responses become intertwined with the ways we learn and teach.

Jesus "Gets" Us

Jesus experienced all human emotions and was acquainted with grief, so he understands and accompanies us through the healing process. In fact, he is the balm for our soul. He knows we also need other people to come alongside us, as we were made for relational connection. If we do not process our negative experiences, we cannot be formed into the identity that God intends us to realize. If we don't address our broken identities healthfully, we will get tangled in negative emotions and false identities that will cloud our living, relating, and teaching and keep us from being vulnerable. Jesus' teaching was vulnerable yet confident, and so can be ours if we understand where we come from, where we are going, and that we are God's beloved. We can't succeed by working harder to change our view of ourselves on our own, but we can instead rely on God to help us to change what we believe about our identity from the inside out.

Pause to Consider:

- What does or would it look like in your life to truly believe you are God's beloved?
- How might an identity clouded by past abuse, rejection, loss, or neglect show up in your teaching or learning?

Our Heritage and Our Identity

Our heritage greatly influences our identity. This affects us

---

[3] David Brooks, *How to Know a Person: The Art of Seeing Others Deeply and Being Deeply Seen* (NY: Random House, 2023), 158.

both individually and as a community. As a Jew, Jesus learned and taught the Old Testament Scriptures, as these were the only scriptures that existed. This background helped shape his human identity, and the Old Testament Scriptures, along with the New Testament Scriptures, should also shape our Christian identity, whether we realize it or not. Lois Tverberg explains:

> The church's lack of knowledge of their own heritage renders much of the wealth of the New Testament inaccessible to them.... I realize that this is a painful metaphor for many of us, but it is, unfortunately, appropriate. The great tragedy of Alzheimer's disease is that it robs a person of themselves by robbing them of their memory of their experiences and relationships. Hence, an elderly woman with Alzheimer's can watch her own children walk through the door and need to ask their names. (As a mother, I cannot imagine the agony of such a state.) The church has a similar condition. Just as the Alzheimer's patient must ask the name of her own children, the church watches her ancestors walk through the door with a similar response. Abraham, Isaac and Jacob are unknown and unnamed. The end result: The church does not know who she is, because she does not know who she was.[4]

---

[4] Lois Tverberg, *Reading the Bible with Rabbi Jesus: How a Jewish Perspective Can Transform Your Understanding* (Ada, MI: Baker Publishing, 2017), loc 2328, Kindle Edition.

Good Bible teachers and students understand the importance of our spiritual heritage, both from the Old Testament Scriptures and from an understanding of church history. A poignant cartoon depicts a school of fish swimming in water, unaware of what water actually is. Likewise, unless we learn our history, we will remain unaware of the ways it shapes our identities and of the waters in which we swim. For those with a Restoration movement church background, my book, *Re-Examining Our Lenses: The Relationship Between Restoration Movement Hermeneutics and Spiritual Formation,* sheds light on ways this background affects our communal and individual identities.[5] When we are more aware of what contributes to our malformed identities, we can then gain confidence that allows for growth and vulnerability.

Identity and Vulnerability

Frederick Buechner speaks of the importance of recognizing the relationship between our identity and our vulnerability as he pens, "The trouble with steeling yourself against the harshness of reality is that the same steel that secures your life against being destroyed secures your life against being opened up and transformed by the holy power that life itself comes from."[6] Author David Brooks adds:

---

[5] Jeanie Shaw, *Re-Examining Our Lenses: The Relationship Between Restoration Movement Hermeneutics and Spiritual Formation* (Spring, TX: Theatron Press, 2024).

[6] Frederick Buechner, *The Sacred Journey* (San Francisco, CA: HarperOne, 2010), 46.

> You can't have a stable identity unless you take the inchoate events of your life and give your life meaning by turning the events into a coherent story. You can know what to do next only if you know what story you are a part of. And you can endure pressure pains only if you can see them as part of a story that will yield future benefits."[7]

Certainly, the gospel account allows us to enter a story of redemption that ends in eternal life with God. Brooks continues with the thought that we are so used to disguising ourselves from others that we often end up disguising ourselves from ourselves.[8] Our identities are wrapped up in our stories, going back generations, and these affect the ways we view ourselves. To transform who we believe we are, we must let God's view of us seep deep within and allow him and others to mirror it back to us. We cannot appreciate our own worth, gifts, and strengths unless they are mirrored back to us from the mind and heart of another. This begins with God. We see ourselves often through the ways others see us. This is why it is so important to realize how Jesus sees us and to teach from that healthy identity.

Pause to Consider:

- Take some time to think of how significant family members viewed you as you grew up. How has this af-

[7] Brooks. *How to Know,* 217.
[8] Brooks. *How to Know,* 224.

fected your identity?

- How does your identity affect the ways you hear input as you learn? What are some ways it can affect your teaching?
- What does it look like to be vulnerable? Do those around you consider you to be vulnerable as you learn and teach?
- What perils more easily befall teachers who struggle with their identity and why? (e.g., ego, stubbornness, difficulty listening, insecurity)

Identity and People Pleasing

Jesus taught from an assured identity as God's beloved (Luke 3:22 NRSV), thus his teaching flowed *out of* his identity; it was not to *gain* an identity. He taught as one who was so at peace with his identity that he was not a people pleaser. Even the Pharisees noted him to be a man with integrity, who taught the way of God in accordance with the truth, paying no attention to who people were or what they thought of him (Mark 12:14). No, Jesus was not a people pleaser. He taught as one who knew he was sent from God and was God; therefore, he taught with the authority of God. He taught as one who knew and understood the Scriptures and how he fulfilled them.

As one who has struggled with pleasing people, I have wrestled with believing that my identity as God's beloved is enough and, as a result, can want to prove my worth. When this happens, what people think can become more important than what God thinks of me. In theory, I know God's view is what defines me, but in practice, I can get off track, concerned about acceptance or what others may be thinking. This description of Jesus as one who pays no attention to who people are but teaches the way of God in accordance with the truth has challenged me and helped me grow. That truth Jesus teaches includes the truth concerning our identity as God's beloved, created in his image. And for Jesus followers, we can rest assured that we have been redeemed by his grace. I can do nothing to earn it, no matter what I accomplish or how carefully I seek to follow him. Remember, motivation that lasts and transforms comes from within.

Throughout my years, speaking up, even when done respectfully, often resulted in strong discipline as a child or in unhealthy retribution as an adult. I remember receiving a belting for stating I did not like the inner gooey part of tomatoes when asked to clean my plate. I soon had trouble knowing or trusting what I felt, especially if it was different from what someone else with power thought. I would thus learn to stuff whatever I felt, and certainly not express it. As an adult, my gender as a woman also contributed to a lack of confidence and a "less than" perspective whenever something I thought or said was deemed of lesser value than a male counterpart's opinion. This also contributed to my hesitance to speak up when someone disagreed with me. I resonated with a scene from the movie *Runaway Bride* where the bride kept running away from the groom on her wedding day(s). It turned out that her running was rooted in her lack of confidence in her identity. The person who finally got through to her and helped her overcome her inability to know and express what she thought had noticed that when at a breakfast diner, she always ordered whatever style of eggs the person she was with ordered.

One day, addressing reasons behind her lack of confidence, her friend told her, "You don't even know how you like your eggs." When I heard that line, I realized, "I have no idea how I like my proverbial eggs." Later in the movie, we see her experience a breakthrough in recognizing and having confidence in her identity. As her friend walks into her home, she has prepared about a dozen different types of eggs. She looks at him and says, "Eggs benedict. I like eggs benedict." I realized that I needed to go much deeper, to the core of my convictions, and act from them, not from what or who others thought I should be. I had to become confident that Jesus is the one I am to please.

If we don't wrestle with finding our healthy, God-given identity, we will tend to think and teach what we think people want to hear. When this happens, it is hard to know how to please Jesus over others. After wrestling long and hard with my identity in Jesus, I have learned to speak up in honesty, but it is still not easy. If I hold to or believe something others might not agree with, I remember the description of Jesus in Mark 12:14. I also remember my dying husband's words to me. He couldn't speak much near the end of his life, but when I shared with him some things I was learning and questioning, he told me, "You will need courage and must decide if you have that courage. I won't be here to help." I have held on to his words of wisdom often. Even more important, I remember that Christ dwells in me through the Spirit. That is enough.

Jesus taught as one so secure of his identity that he could teach what was uncomfortable while remaining a vulnerable servant to those who opposed or betrayed him. He taught as one who embodied love, as this was his identity, since God is love (1 John 4:8), and Jesus is the exact representation of God (Hebrews 1:3).

We are not Jesus, though we follow him. While Jesus knew he was God, we are certainly not—though we can be sure that we are created in God's image. Since the Spirit enters to dwell in us at our spiritual birth, we become divine beings (2 Peter 1:4) who, amazingly, have been given the mind of Christ (1 Corinthians 2:16). We have unique personalities, backgrounds, and learning styles, and we relate, teach, and learn from these. We project who we are and how we think to those we teach, like it or not. It is hard to be detached from unhealthy identities, so knowing ourselves is crucial to teaching. Once we are more aware of the identities we hold to, we can then let Jesus transform them from the lies we believe about ourselves to the truth Jesus tells us about ourselves.

Pause to Consider:

- Do you agree that knowing yourself is crucial to teaching? Why or why not?
- Consider what lies Satan tells you about yourself as compared to the identity Jesus gives you. What are some of the lies?

- Once you become more aware of the identity you hold to that hinders you, will you let the Spirit replace the lies with truths? What are those truths?
- When negative tapes play in your head, how might you reframe them to match who God says you are?

Embodied Identities

Teaching involves more than words. Though God gave commandments and spoke through the prophets of old, he knew we needed a flesh-and-blood example to follow. The best teachers live what they teach; that is a part of what makes Jesus the Master Teacher. As we teach, we are embodied teachers teaching embodied students. This embodiment is part of our identity, involving physical, emotional, and spiritual dimensions. Parker Palmer describes the connection between good teaching and our understanding of our identity:

> Good teaching cannot be reduced to technique; good teaching comes from the identity and integrity of the teacher.... In every story I have heard, good teachers share one trait; a strong sense of personal identity infuses their work. "Dr. A is really there when she teaches,"...or "Mr. B has such an enthusiasm for his subject,"...or "You can tell that this is really Prof. C's life."[9]

---

[9] Parker J. Palmer, "The Heart of a Teacher: Identity and Integrity in Teaching," *Change: The Magazine of Higher Learning* 1997, 29 (6): 14–21. doi:10.1080/00091389709602343. Published online March 25, 2010, https://www.tandfonline.com/doi/abs/10.1080/00091389709602343.

Palmer continues:

> Bad teachers distance themselves from the subject they are teaching—and in the process from their students.... As we try to connect ourselves and our subjects with our students, we make ourselves, as well as our subjects, vulnerable to indifference, judgment, and ridicule. To reduce our vulnerability, we disconnect from students, from subjects, and even from ourselves. We build a wall between inner truth and outer performance, and we "play-act" the teacher's part. Our words, spoken and removed from our hearts, become "the balloon speech in cartoons," and we become caricatures of ourselves.[10]

Palmer reminds that power works from the outside in, but true authority works from the inside out:

> The clue is in the word itself, which has "author" at its core. Authority is thus granted to people who are perceived as "authoring" their own words, actions, their own lives, rather than playing a scripted role removed from their own hearts. When teachers depend on the coercive powers of law or technique, they have no authority at all.[11]

---

[10] Palmer, "The Heart."
[11] Palmer, "The Heart."

Authority is not control, but comes from the surety of who Jesus is and who we are. The writer of Hebrews describes Jesus as the author and finisher of our faith. His teaching came from who he was. He was true to God, so he could be true to himself. No wonder we are to fix our eyes on him.

> Therefore, since we have so great a cloud of witnesses surrounding us, let us also lay aside every encumbrance and the sin which so easily entangles us, and let us run with endurance the race that is set before us, fixing our eyes on Jesus, the author and perfecter of faith, who for the joy set before Him endured the cross, despising the shame, and has sat down at the right hand of the throne of God.
>
> For consider Him who has endured such hostility by sinners against Himself, so that you will not grow weary and lose heart. (Hebrews12:1–3 NASB1995)

Jesus continually taught what was true, impervious to criticism or rejection, because he knew who he was, where he had come from, and where he was going. And because he desires us to be with him, he would not be deterred by things that often entangle us. Amazingly, his *hesed* (steadfast love) entreats us to follow him as citizens of the kingdom of heaven, even while we are on earth. Thus, he taught us to pray, "Your kingdom come, your will be done, on earth as it is in heaven" (Matthew 6:10).

Staying in the Room

During my training as a spiritual director, my supervisors were not so concerned with what I said to those I "directed,"[12] but rather, they focused on what was going on inside me as I listened to those I directed. This is the role of the supervisor. When my conversations with someone I am directing trigger inner thoughts in me, this is termed "leaving the room." We can be in the same room with people as teachers or students and still "leave the room," distracted by what is going on inside us, even while physically remaining with them. The more aware we are of our inner thoughts and conflicts, the more balanced our teaching and living become. When we become entangled because of our misconstrued identities, we cannot be fully present for another.

Pause to Consider:

- When are times in your teaching, listening, or learning that you have "left the room"?
- What kinds of inner thoughts and conflicts caused you to "leave the room"?
- Reflect on ways your inner thoughts and conflicts affect you as you teach or learn.

---

[12] I put "directing" in quotes, because spiritual direction is much more about walking alongside a person, helping them find and notice God in their journey than it is about directing. Surprisingly because of the name of the practice of spiritual direction, my coaching practice employs more "direction" than my practice of spiritual direction.

Insecurity and Identity

Insecurity reigns when we are not confident of who we really are or whose we are. We may then try to prove or earn our worth through what we do or what we have. We will find it difficult to be vulnerable, in case others might come to know the real us. We might shut down or seek to fit in and be accepted, all of which affects our teaching and, really, all aspects of life. When we become confident in our identity, we can then speak with confidence. In Luke 2:49, when Jesus as a twelve-year-old was conversing with the elders and teachers of the law, he asked his parents, "Why were you searching for me?" … "Didn't you know I had to be in my Father's house?" He knew where he came from and where he was going. Is our true home "our Father's house"? Jesus' proclamation, "Even if I testify on my own behalf, my testimony is valid, for I know where I came from and where I am going" expresses a profound identity. Let that marinate a while.

Identity and Humility

If we know where we come from and where we are going, humility can then flow from the inside out. True humility cannot be manufactured, thus when we try to fill what feels lacking in our sense of identity, we become self-protective, and false humility abounds. To grow in humility, I believe it crucial to gain a healed sense of identity, knowing where we truly come from and where we are going. Then we will know we belong to and are truly loved by God, which breeds humility.

As God, Jesus had to learn what it was like to be human. This took humility. He chose to learn how we as humans breathe, eat, walk, grow, hurt, cry, despair, rejoice, share friendship, and finally die. Jesus grew in wisdom, in physical stature, and in relationships (Luke 2:52). He learned by asking questions of the elders while in the temple (Luke 2:41–47). He watched and learned from nature, from culture, from individuals, and from people groups. He taught from what he learned from all these. He learned facts, but he also learned humans, whom the facts are for. He also learned obedience through suffering (Hebrews 5:8).

Job had once lamented to God:

> "Do you have eyes of flesh?
>   Do you see as a mortal sees?
> Are your days like those of a mortal
>   or your years like those of a strong man,
> that you must search out my faults
>   and probe after my sin?" (Job 10:3–8)

Though God was silent with Job when the latter spoke, God eventually answered him with the living Word, Jesus. God incarnate. God who became human, with eyes of flesh, seeing as mortals see. He could then tell Job, "Yes, Job, I do have eyes of flesh. I have experienced mortality. I know." This tells me that even God himself learned by becoming human.

Pause to Consider:

- How does knowing where we come from and where we are going breed humility?
- How do you think a healthy view of identity can help you be humble?
- What does manufactured humility (false humility) look like?

Humility will present the same whether we are teachers or students. If we are humble, we will always be students. By nature of what it means to teach, teachers often hold more knowledge than some others, and humility can prove more difficult for them. Listening is a mark of humility. Humility is required to fully listen to another's thoughts without formulating a response while "listening." Humility is open to being wrong. Humility encourages avid reading that can grow and challenge our current understanding as we compare such learning with God's ways. I have been humbled by things I have learned in my theological studies and training as I realize, more than ever, how much I do not know.

Jesus defined humility with his life and through his teachings. Philippians 2 describes the qualities of his humility. This collection of verses put into a "chapter" was likely an early Christian hymn:

> Do nothing out of selfish ambition or vain conceit. Rather, in humility value others above yourselves, not looking to your

own interests but each of you to the interests of the others.

In your relationships with one another, have the same mindset as Christ Jesus:

Who, being in very nature God,
did not consider equality with God
something to be used to his own advantage;
rather, he made himself nothing
by taking the very nature of a servant,
being made in human likeness.
And being found in appearance as a man,
he humbled himself
by becoming obedient to death—
even death on a cross!
Therefore God exalted him to the highest place
and gave him the name that is above every name,
that at the name of Jesus every knee should bow,
in heaven and on earth and under the earth,
and every tongue acknowledge that Jesus Christ is
Lord, to the glory of God the Father.

(Philippians 2:3–11)

Without humility, while teachers may offer valuable information, their teaching is rendered empty, if not disingenuous. Quite often, trained Bible teachers are gifted with exceptional intelligence. This gift can sometimes be accompanied by social difficulties, and humility means one is eager to learn, letting others help. As my eleven-year-old friend Charlie wisely explained, "A nerd is social and smart, a geek is smart but not social, and a dork is not smart or social." So it would seem teachers need a good dose of "nerdship" rather than "geekiness" *or* "dorkdom." For everyone, a good posture of humility is one that acknowledges, "I need to learn, and I need you."

Pause to Consider:

- How do you demonstrate letting Jesus (and people) know that you need them?
- Think of interactions with your spouse, your family members, your colleagues, those you teach, your teachers, and even those who are hard to get along with. How might the humility that describes Jesus (in Philippians 2) apply?

Humility Learns, Listens, and Is Vulnerable

We know that Jesus was raised in the Jewish culture, which valued and studied the Scriptures. Deuteronomy contains what is known as the Shema prayer (Deuteronomony 6:4–6), which we learn from history was spoken throughout the day in a typical Jewish family. It was customary for a family to consistently talk about and recite scriptures together. According to the Mishnah, Avot 3:4, "When three eat at one table and words of Torah are not spoken there, it is as if they ate at the altars of the dead.... But when three eat at one table and bring up words of Torah, it is as if they ate from the table of God!"[13] They believed

[13] Attributed to Rabbi Simeon ben Yohai, who lived between AD100 and 160.

the study of God's word invokes his presence and makes the gathering holy. Jesus would likely have followed this tradition. Humility does not assume that once I hear or teach something that "I'm good." Humility knows the need to be reminded of God's presence and pre-eminence. Jesus did not teach something as "one and done." He was a master at spaced repetition, teaching truths in varied ways to help the learners understand and apply the teaching.

In the prophecies of Isaiah, the suffering servant speaks of learning and teaching:

> The LORD God has given me
>   the tongue of a teacher,
> that I may know how to sustain
>   the weary with a word.
> Morning by morning he wakens—
>   wakens my ear
>   to listen as those who are taught.
> The LORD God has opened my ear,
>   and I was not rebellious,
>   I did not turn backward." (Isaiah 50:4–5 NRSV)

Certainly, Jesus embodied an ear attuned to his Father. He listened. Humility demonstrates a vulnerability that allows others into our lives and lets us be instructed, morning by morning. Without an ear eager to listen and learn, morning by morning, we will be spiritually and relationally hard of hearing.

Pause to Consider:

- Speaking Scripture from memory helps remind us of what is important and encourages humility. Try speaking the Shema prayer or the greatest commandment as a part of your day for a week. Consider whether this might be a helpful tool to incorporate into your life on a daily basis.

Identity and Emotions

Jesus, though the Master Teacher, was also vulnerable with his emotions. While facing his greatest challenge as he prayed in the garden before his death, he vulnerably expressed his need for the support of his friends. In this, he taught several valuable lessons. Teaching is not absent from emotions, and teaching does not necessarily involve a pulpit. It more often involves humble, vulnerable conversations. We will not be able to express the need for others if we are not first clear on our identity, and then are humble enough to say, "I need you." Jesus, in his humanity, understood vulnerability yet continually gave his heart to people who hurt or neglected him in his hour of need.

> Then Jesus went with his disciples to a place called Gethsemane, and he said to them, "Sit here while I go over there and pray." He took Peter and the two sons of Zebedee along with him, and he began to be sorrowful and troubled. Then he said to them, "My soul is overwhelmed with sorrow to the point of death. Stay here and keep watch with me."

> Going a little farther, he fell with his face to the ground and prayed, "My Father, if it is possible, may this cup be taken from me. Yet not as I will, but as you will."
>
> Then he returned to his disciples and found them sleeping. "Couldn't you men keep watch with me for one hour?" he asked Peter. (Matthew 26:36–40)

In this instance, he taught his students the need for vulnerability and trust. Then, while on the cross, he taught perhaps his most poignant lesson. Looking at those who mocked, tortured, and betrayed him, he somehow found the words, "Father, forgive them, for they do not know what they are doing" (Luke 23:34). This requires a level of humility and vulnerability beyond imagination.

After Jesus was resurrected, he chose to entrust his message and ministry to men and women, many of whom had recently denied him. This is a vulnerable trust and can only come from a humble servant who knows who he is and how great is God. When we understand where we come from, and who we come from, humility becomes possible.

Identity, Humility, and Awe

Rabbi Abraham Heschel declares that modern readers lack the ability to appreciate the grandeur of God. Without this appreciation, teachers, along with all people, will lack humility.

Heschel explains:

> Greeks learned in order to comprehend. Hebrews learned in order to revere. The modern man learns in order to use.... To the modern man everything seems calculable; everything reducible to a figure. He has supreme faith in statistics and abhors the idea of a mystery. Obstinately he ignores the fact that we are all surrounded by things which we apprehend but cannot comprehend; that even reason is a mystery to itself. He is sure of his ability to explain all mystery away.
>
> The awareness of grandeur and the sublime is all but gone from the modern mind.... The sense for the sublime, the sign of the inward greatness of the human soul and something which is potentially given to all men, is now a rare gift. Yet without it, the world becomes flat and the soul a vacuum.[14]

Our theology often teaches that humans are very big, and God is very far away. This view resists humility, because our understanding of our identity is lacking. When our identity is connected to the understanding that we are created in God's image and are beloved by him, and that he dwells in us, we can then be free to let go of self-dependence and cast all our trust on him.

Perhaps one of the most misunderstood aspects of humility is a lack of understanding about what I cannot do apart from recognizing the source of life, where I come from. Jesus, God in

---

[14] Abraham Joshua Heschel, *God in Search of Man* (NY: Ferrar, Straus, and Giroux, 1955), 36, as cited in Tverberg, *Reading the Bible.*

the flesh, said:

> "For as the Father has life in himself, so he has granted the Son also to have life in himself. And he has given him authority to judge because he is the Son of Man.
>
> "Do not be amazed at this, for a time is coming when all who are in their graves will hear his voice and come out—those who have done what is good will rise to live, and those who have done what is evil will rise to be condemned. By myself I can do nothing; I judge only as I hear, and my judgment is just, for I seek not to please myself but him who sent me." (John 5:26–30)

While apart from Christ, we can do nothing. In him, we are given that life that cannot be snuffed out. Life that is eternal and abundant. With him, all things are possible. As Paul confesses, "I can do all things through him who strengthens me" (Philippians 4:13 NRSV).

Life-Giving Identity

Because Jesus has life in himself from the Father, he can grant us living water that wells up into eternal life (John 4:14). This life authored in Jesus lets us know and experience where we come from and where we are going. Later on, John recounts Jesus' discourse on the vine and branches that further explains this source of life:

Remain in me, as I also remain in you. No branch can bear fruit by itself; it must remain in the vine. Neither can you bear fruit unless you remain in me.

"I am the vine; you are the branches. If you remain in me and I in you, you will bear much fruit; apart from me you can do nothing. If you do not remain in me, you are like a branch that is thrown away and withers; such branches are picked up, thrown into the fire and burned. If you remain in me and my words remain in you, ask whatever you wish, and it will be done for you. This is to my Father's glory, that you bear much fruit, showing yourselves to be my disciples.

"As the Father has loved me, so have I loved you. Now remain in my love. If you keep my commands, you will remain in my love, just as I have kept my Father's commands and remain in his love. I have told you this so that my joy may be in you and that your joy may be complete. My command is this: Love each other as I have loved you. Greater love has no one than this: to lay down one's life for one's friends. You are my friends if you do what I command. I no longer call you servants, because a servant does not know his master's business. Instead, I have called you friends, for everything that I learned from my Father I have made known to you. You did not choose me, but I chose you and appointed you so that you might go and bear fruit—fruit that will last—and so that whatever you ask in my name the Father will give you. This is my command: Love each other. (John 15:4–17)

Some of us more easily read this passage as if it contains a punitive threat (if you don't remain in me, I will throw you away), as well as a charge to "bear fruit." Jesus never says he will throw us away, but instead he longs for us to remain with and in him so that we won't shrivel up and die and someone else throws us out. The tone of this teaching, when we read it in context, is about love and relationship. It is about abiding or "being," rather than doing. The punitive, self-focused interpretation also puts emphasis on what we do, our efforts, proving our worthiness as disciples. I often (mis)used these verses to stress the importance of keeping God's commands and the need to bear fruit. This would be as ridiculous as my standing outside by my grapevine near my back door and yelling at it to "produce." Instead, it needs nurturing and care, then the grapes happen.

While I believe obeying God is crucial and right, the message on abiding is about God's love and friendship, and the lifestyle or "fruit" then flows out of that relationship. Jesus also notes that our relationship with him is meant to bring complete joy (v.11), not angst over precise obedience. It takes humility to forgo self-dependence and personal effort in understanding our identity. Humility breeds an understanding that I cannot change my heart or actions on my own or by my strongest willpower. I must let God change me from the inside, which is scary, because I cannot control this. I must rely on God's power. May God give us the humility to know where we come from and where we are going, and thus able to abide in him.

Pause to Consider:

- How do you view the relationship between humility, vulnerability, and your understanding of your identity—where you come from and where you are going?
- How might you foster the acceptance that you are created in God's image and beloved by him, and that he dwells in you? How might this affect your humility? How might this show up in the ways you teach?

My favorite teacher taught me how to ask questions. There is power to learning when you are not afraid to ask questions and dig (research) on your own. Question everything and you will find truth if you dig deep enough. – Kimberly

Storytelling really draws me in. – Derek

Their only agenda is helping you learn. They teach in creative ways, with an emphasis on getting you to think and not just memorize facts. – Ed

My best teacher had vision for our success [and taught us] to love reading, that we could get more out of a book than the surface story, to read between the lines, to listen carefully to the author's voice. He also taught us self-respect at a deep level, and deeper respect for others. – Nancy

The best teachers modeled what they expected from their students. They were well-versed, lifelong learners and developed in us a love of learning by sharing from their own experiences. – Susan

They make difficult concepts accessible, connecting head and heart for life-changing, Aha! moments. They are humble and reliant on God in the Spirit—teaching is the overflow of their relationship with their Abba Father. – Matina

They opened my eyes to a world of possibilities I never could have dreamed of at that particular point in life. I learned confidence and began to explore a world outside the small hometown and insular family life where I had existed my entire life up to that point. – Bonnie

The professor expected us to find the answers, stimulating us to think deeply and learn for ourselves, not just repeat what he said. He wanted to stimulate thought. – Ryan

Chapter Three

The Master Teacher as Philosopher

Jesus, the Master Teacher, was more than a teacher. Accompanying his credentials of rabbi, teacher, Son of God, Son of Man, redeemer, giver of life, overcomer of death, Jesus would have been considered a philosopher. But he was not like other philosophers. Other philosophers, already known for centuries during Jesus' lifetime, offered lofty teachings and ideals but led lifestyles less than righteous. These include philosophers such as Socrates (with his affection for young boys), along with Aristotle (who had deep-rooted disrespect for women), and Plato. Jesus was different in the way he lived. He remained full of integrity and without sin, not to mention the fact that he was raised from the dead. That changes everything. Unlike many famous philosophers, he lived a life worthy of full imitation.

In *Jesus Through Middle Eastern Eyes,* theologian Kenneth Bailey offers a nuance to Jesus as a philosopher, stating that Jesus "created meaning like a dramatist and a poet rather than like a philosopher." Bailey describes Jesus as a "metaphorical theologian" whose "primary method of creating meaning was through metaphor, simile, parable and dramatic action rather than through logic and reasoning."[15] Jesus seemed to perfectly combine all these methods of teaching, knowing we all have different ways we learn and that we need all of these. As a philosopher, Jesus did not teach by simply giving important facts. His teachings instructed people how to think.

As I write this chapter, I have recently returned from a trip to Antioch in Turkey, where several 2023 earthquakes devastated the city, killing over 53,000 people. It was sobering to witness, and as our tour guide explained, so many structures were lost because they were built on unstable soil. As I walked through ancient ruins amid the year-old ruins, I could almost picture walking with Jesus down those broken roads as he looked around at the collapsed structures and reminded those with him what Matthew recorded in chapter 7:24–27. Here, he instructs people how to think using metaphors, pictures, stories, logic, and reasoning.

> "Everyone then who hears these words of mine and does them will be like a wise man who built his house on the rock. And the rain fell, and the floods came, and the winds blew and beat on that house, but it did not fall, because it had been founded on the rock. And everyone who hears these words of mine and does not do them will be like a foolish man who built his house on the sand. And the rain fell, and the floods came, and the winds blew and beat against that house, and it fell, and great was the fall of it." (ESV)

---

[15] Kenneth Bailey, *Jesus Through Middle Eastern Eyes: Cultural Studies in the Gospels* (Downers Grove, IL: InterVarsity Press, 2008), 279.

As he completes his teaching, I picture his audience reacting with astonishment at his wise words. He reaches into their core values, addressing their fundamental beliefs in life. He knew that if people did not live life from their deepest core convictions, their actions would become unsustainable "add-ons." Structures built on sand. He knew those core convictions must be solid, founded in the unshakable principles of the kingdom of heaven.

Evaluating the Premises on Which We Build

During my first spiritual formation graduate class, I was asked to recount and record my core values for an assignment. This was a meaningful exercise, as we evaluated our core values concerning faith formation, emotional formation, social/interpersonal formation, health and wellness formation, theological/intellectual formation, vocational formation, and resources stewardship. I evaluated my core values in each of these areas as honestly as I could and recorded them on paper. I realized that these values form the belief system from which I live. I also realized that if the way I was living was not congruent with my core values, then something was amiss that needed to change. I was asked to support these values with scriptures and describe their application to my life. The exercise caused me to re-evaluate several of them, especially concerning health and wellness and resources stewardship. I realized that if my lifestyle did not demonstrate the core values I espoused, I needed to change either my values or my lifestyle. Since my values are rooted in

God's word, the choice called for me to change my way of living.

As a result of evaluating my core values on health and wellness, I began exercising regularly, ate more healthfully, strengthened my core muscles, and lost forty pounds. This came as a result of evaluating my core convictions alongside the ways I live. When I realized that God's values and mine concerning resources and stewardship did not fully match, I began caring for the earth in deeper ways, taking seriously things such as recycling and using sustainable products. I had not previously addressed core values in this area of life. I am still discerning how to more fully practice hospitality to the poor and marginalized because of this exercise, and I am sure I still have things to change. This evaluation still helps me to determine whether the ways I live match the core values I espouse. A discernment exercise such as this can help us evaluate how we use our time and money, offer hospitality, and much more. Jesus' teaching reached into people's hearts and core values, seeking to transform them from their innermost being.

Jesus said in Luke 6:45, "The good man out of the good treasure of his heart brings forth what is good; and the evil man out of the evil treasure brings forth what is evil; for his mouth speaks from that which fills his heart" (NASB1995). We can't truly change our actions without evaluating and living out of our core beliefs. It is simply unsustainable and will eventually crash when the earthquakes (or lifequakes) come.

The values of our heart affect the actions we take and the words we speak.

Consider a few of Jesus' teachings for several areas mentioned:

Faith Formation

In the Gospels, we see Jesus' amazement at the centurion's faith (Matthew 8:5–13) and we also see him amazed at the lack of faith from those in his hometown (Mark 6:6). Faith accompanied Jesus' healings and forgiving of sins. After Jesus' resurrection, when Thomas asked to see Jesus' hands and feet, Jesus allowed him to do so. How I appreciate Jesus' words that tell us he understands that faith formation is harder when we have not seen him physically; yet when we do believe we will be blessed.

> A week later his disciples were in the house again, and Thomas was with them. Though the doors were locked, Jesus came and stood among them and said, "Peace be with you!" Then he said to Thomas, "Put your finger here; see my hands. Reach out your hand and put it into my side. Stop doubting and believe."
>
> Thomas said to him, "My Lord and my God!"
>
> Then Jesus told him, "Because you have seen me, you have believed; blessed are those who have not seen and yet have believed." (John 20:26–29)

Perhaps Jesus' words that most describe faith formation come when he asks Peter if he wishes to leave and no longer follow him. Our core convictions about faith will determine our lifelong followership. At our core, we must answer the question,

"Who else has the words of eternal life?"

> The Spirit gives life; the flesh counts for nothing. The words I have spoken to you—they are full of the Spirit and life. Yet there are some of you who do not believe." For Jesus had known from the beginning which of them did not believe and who would betray him. He went on to say, "This is why I told you that no one can come to me unless the Father has enabled them."
>
> From this time many of his disciples turned back and no longer followed him.
>
> "You do not want to leave too, do you?" Jesus asked the Twelve.
>
> Simon Peter answered him, "Lord, to whom shall we go? You have the words of eternal life. We have come to believe and to know that you are the Holy One of God." (John 6:63–69)

Jesus offers his followers choice, but faith comes from knowing that Jesus is the author of eternal life, which can be found nowhere else.

Emotional Formation

One need not look further than Jesus' Sermon on the Mount to discover his profound teaching on core beliefs concerning emotions. As anxiety, worry, and malformed identity plague our emotional wellness, Jesus offers truths that counter the emotional baggage we carry. He reminds us that the things we carry begin from the core of our belief system as he teaches, "A good tree cannot bear bad fruit, and a bad tree cannot bear good fruit" (Matthew 7:18).

Addressing worry, he says,

> "Therefore I tell you, do not worry about your life, what you will eat or drink; or about your body, what you will wear. Is not life more than food, and the body more than clothes? Look at the birds of the air; they do not sow or reap or store away in barns, and yet your heavenly Father feeds them. Are you not much more valuable than they? Can any one of you by worrying add a single hour to your life?
>
> "And why do you worry about clothes? See how the flowers of the field grow. They do not labor or spin. Yet I tell you that not even Solomon in all his splendor was dressed like one of these. If that is how God clothes the grass of the field, which is here today and tomorrow is thrown into the fire, will he not much more clothe you—you of little faith? So do not worry, saying, 'What shall we eat?' or 'What shall we drink?' or 'What shall we wear?' For the pagans run after all these things, and your heavenly Father knows that you need them. But seek first his kingdom and his righteousness, and all these things will be given to you as well. Therefore do not worry about tomorrow, for tomorrow will worry about itself. Each day has enough trouble of its own. (Matthew 6:25–34)

Jesus' teachings recognize and authenticate the gamut of

human emotion, but he counters the hurtful emotions Satan wants to use against us with a new way to view them. His alternate view offers a life-giving, transformative way to think that results in our being blessed. Jesus' heart is to bless us. In fact, God's first words to humankind were to bless them (Genesis 1:27–28), and interestingly, Jesus' last words to humankind were also a blessing (Luke 24:50–52). He spoke this blessing as he ascended. This is Jesus' heart for his beloved: to bless.

> Now when Jesus saw the crowds, he went up on a mountainside and sat down. His disciples came to him, and he began to teach them.
>
> He said:
>
> "Blessed are the poor in spirit,
> for theirs is the kingdom of heaven.
> Blessed are those who mourn,
> for they will be comforted.
> Blessed are the meek,
> for they will inherit the earth.
> Blessed are those who hunger and thirst
> for righteousness,
> for they will be filled.
> Blessed are the merciful,
> for they will be shown mercy.
> Blessed are the pure in heart,
> for they will see God.
> Blessed are the peacemakers,
> for they will be called children of God.

> Blessed are those who are persecuted
> because of righteousness,
> for theirs is the kingdom of heaven.
>
> "Blessed are you when people insult you, persecute you and falsely say all kinds of evil against you because of me. Rejoice and be glad, because great is your reward in heaven, for in the same way they persecuted the prophets who were before you. (Matthew 5:1–12)

Jesus understands human emotions, participated in them, and offers the kingdom-of-heaven perspective that can transform our thinking and our emotions so we can find fulfillment, peace, comfort, mercy, eternal life, and all-around blessings.

Social/Interpersonal Formation

Jesus' teachings were not just for individual blessings; they were also meant to heal the relationships broken ever since sin entered the world. Sin brought jealousy, discord, favoritism, the desire to dominate, hatred, murder, and all sorts of "isms" to relational connections, or disconnections. Jesus' teachings are meant to touch the core of our beliefs in ways that change how we relate to each other. Certainly, Jesus shared the foundational premise for relational connection as he instructed us to love our neighbors as ourselves (Matthew 22:39) and taught, "In everything, do to others what you would have them do to you, for this sums up the Law and the Prophets" (Matthew 7:12). Love is at the core of Jesus' foundational teachings, and only with such foundational convictions can people find the unity he longed for and prayed for. Only through love will people be recognized as followers of Jesus. He teaches such: "A new commandment I give to you, that you love one another: just as I have loved you, you also are to love one another. By this all people will know you are my disciples, if you have love for one another." (John 13:34-35 ESV). Without love, as Paul notes, we are but noisy gongs and clanging cymbals (1 Corinthians 13:1). Jesus' teaching reaches to the core of our relational connections.

Health and Wellness Formation

Jesus tells his disciples, "Come with me by yourselves to a quiet place and get some rest" (Mark 6:31). This was because there were so many people coming and going that they didn't have time to eat. He knew, even with a mission to accomplish, that the body needs physical and emotional rest.

In Matthew 11:28 Jesus teaches, "Come to me, all you who are weary and burdened, and I will give you rest. Take my yoke upon you and learn from me, for I am gentle and humble in heart, and you will find rest for your souls."

Life was different during Jesus' days, as walking was the main way of travel. Certainly, this would have benefited the health of the travelers, as would partaking of unprocessed foods, since they ate from the land. Sickness and death remain in our fallen world, and Jesus shows his redeemed plan for health and wellness as he begins his ministry. In his teachings, he points to a resurrected life that no disease or human intervention can destroy. He begins his ministry reading from Isaiah:

> "The Spirit of the Lord is on me,
> because he has anointed me
> to proclaim good news to the poor.
> He has sent me to proclaim freedom for the prisoners
> and recovery of sight for the blind,
> to set the oppressed free,
> to proclaim the year of the Lord's favor." (Luke 4:18–19)

Resource Stewardship

Much of Jesus' teaching showed concern for the poor. He warned of the dangers of greed and the love of money. Even so, resources were meant to be used and increased, as taught in the Parable of the Talents. In Matthew 25:14–29 is recorded one of Jesus' parables that teaches the importance of investing the resources entrusted to us so they can be increasingly useful. But Jesus doesn't teach a "prosperity gospel"; far from it. He teaches his followers:

> "Do not store up for yourselves treasures on earth, where moths and vermin destroy, and where thieves break in and steal. But store up for yourselves treasures in heaven, where moths and vermin do not destroy, and where thieves do not break in and steal. For where your treasure is, there your heart will be also.
>
> "The eye is the lamp of the body. If your eyes are

> healthy, your whole body will be full of light. But if your eyes are unhealthy, your whole body will be full of darkness. If then the light within you is darkness, how great is that darkness!" (Matthew 6:19–23)

He instructs concerning our attitudes for stewardship as it relates to giving:

> "So when you give to the needy, do not announce it with trumpets, as the hypocrites do in the synagogues and on the streets, to be honored by others. Truly I tell you, they have received their reward in full. But when you give to the needy, do not let your left hand know what your right hand is doing, so that your giving may be in secret. Then your Father, who sees what is done in secret, will reward you." (Matthew 6:2–4)

While these principles apply to Jesus' teachings on core values concerning resource stewardship, these same values would also be applicable as we evaluate our foundational beliefs concerning our vocations. When they align with God's kingdom values, our whole body will be full of light.

Pause to Consider:

- Consider the core values you currently hold; not necessarily values you think you should have. Core values can be ascertained by discerning the beliefs that determine your choices, your thought processes, and your actions. This is not a quick exercise, but it can serve you well. There is plenty of room for growth and adjustment, but it is important to evaluate the values you hold. Those are the ones that most affect the ways you process life and relationships. For example:

Faith Formation: What are some of Jesus' teachings that inform my core values concerning my faith?

What are my top two core values concerning my faith?

Emotional Formation: What are some of Jesus' teachings that inform my core values concerning my emotional formation?

What are my top two core values concerning my emotional formation?

Social/Interpersonal Formation: What are some of Jesus' teachings that inform my core values concerning my relational formation?

What are my top two core values concerning my social/interpersonal formation?

Theological/Intellectual Formation: What are some of Jesus' teachings that inform my core values concerning my intellectual formation?

What are my top two core values concerning my theological/ intellectual formation?

Vocation: What are some of Jesus' teachings that inform my core values concerning my vocational formation?

What are my top two core values concerning my vocational formation?

Health and Wellness: What are some of Jesus' teachings that inform my core values concerning my health and wellness formation?

What are my top two core values concerning my health and wellness formation?

Resource Stewardship: What are some of Jesus' teachings that inform my core values concerning my resource stewardship formation?

What are my top two core values concerning resource stewardship?

Jesus and the Big Life Questions

Today, the study of philosophy would include the views of the likes of Aristotle, Plato, Kant, and others, but likely would not include those of Jesus. The word "philosophy" has changed meaning over time. In *Jesus the Great Philosopher,* Jonathan Pennington notes ways in which this change has affected the church, and too often Christian teaching, because faith can easily be disconnected from other aspects of life, such as the ones we just evaluated. This results in people looking to other sources for life's wisdom rather than to Jesus. Modern day "philosophers" have huge Instagram followings, but their life and credentials cannot touch the life of Jesus. Nor were they raised from the dead. That's rather a big deal!

Jesus asked the big questions the Scriptures seek to answer, but too often we fail to learn what he teaches concerning the big philosophical, core-value questions. We often learn (and teach) rational, scientific facts that fail to address deep belief systems concerning how the world works, how people relate, and how we are to live in the world. Pennington describes this dilemma:

> Christians believe in the authority of Scripture, but often fail to ask the questions of the Bible that God seeks to answer. Teachers have too often stopped asking the relational, philosophical questions: What is reality? What does it mean to be human? How do we find happiness? Why do we suffer? What is the meaning of hope?[16]

While all kinds of biblical teachings are needed, when we don't wrestle with these big questions and discern the divine and spiritual realm, we fail to address the questions and

---

[16] Jonathan T. Pennington, *Jesus the Great Philosopher: Rediscovering the Wisdom Needed for the Good Life* (Grand Rapids, MI: Brazos Press, 2020), 15.

thoughts in which people most want to engage. This limits our effectiveness with the world and with the younger generation in the church, as these are the questions that burn in their hearts.

Philosophers, Teachers, and Models

Ancient philosophers were also considered teachers, but they were teachers who engaged these questions. Pennington continues, telling us that people looked to philosophers to make sense of the world, the cosmos, and relationships. This is why they were so important. He explains that the goal of ancient philosophy was to love wisdom and love the good.[17] He pens, "Understanding how the world is constructed and functions (physics) teaches us who we are [and] what the nature of truth and time and being are (metaphysics), and this enables us to live well."[18] He tells us that teachers/philosophers also concerned themselves with how we know things (epistemology), how we live out what is right (ethics), and how best to structure society and institutions (politics).[19]

This way of studying became a sort of ancient spiritual formation, concerned with spiritual growth and responding to different aspects of philosophy. As philosopher Pierre Hadot describes, "Thus, ancient philosophies can be described as 'spiritual exercises' or life practices informed and formed by reflections for the building of practical wisdom in one's inner-

---

[17] Pennington, *Jesus,* 22.
[18] Pennington, *Jesus,* 23.
[19] Pennington, *Jesus,* 28.

most self."[20]

Ancient philosophers were not simply teachers, but were also seen as models in community who had the training, life experience, and capacity combined with virtue and integrity to serve as instructors and models.[21] They were vital to spiritual life. Hadot notes that philosophy was carried out in schools with conversations and life models between masters and disciples and was a way of life. I find it helpful to better understand the thinking that Jesus would have encountered as a Master Teacher by better understanding the kind of teaching with which people in his day were most familiar. The role of a teacher is different in today's Western culture. Today, teaching modes have become more about delivering facts and knowledge. And these teachers are ubiquitous. When we don't know something today, we google it. Certainly, we can learn much from Jesus' comprehensive teaching, which doesn't ignore facts but recognizes that all Scripture and facts of science and nature are meant to lead us to what is truly important, a relationship with him.

Finding the Good Life Jesus' Way

After the time of the Enlightenment, when rational teaching and scientific facts became key, philosophy and virtuous living became separate entities. Physics became the study of cosmology, ethics became religion, language became linguistics,

---

[20] Pierre Hadot, *What Is Ancient Philosophy?* Eng trans of 1995 French ed "What Is Ancient Philosophy?" trans. Michael Chase (Cambridge, MA: Belknap, 2004), 6.
[21] Pennington, *Jesus,* 19.

and human habits were moved to the study of neuroscience and psychology. Today, the study of philosophy differs greatly from ancient studies. The study of modern philosophy has become a survey of philosophy's history. Pennington concurs:

> Religion in the ancient world was not primarily a set of beliefs to be cognitively acknowledged, but an allegiance to a certain God or gods that showed you how to see the world and how to be in the world so that you might find life.... Philosophy was allegiance to a certain way of seeing and being in the world, learned and lived in community for the purpose of finding the Good Life.[22]

These nuances become important when learning about Jesus, the Master Teacher. The Greek philosophical schools were models for the rabbinic schools of Jesus' day; thus, the Hebrew Scriptures present themselves as a work of ancient philosophy divinely revealed. Orthodox Israeli scholar Yoram Hazony notes that the idea that a book can't be considered philosophy because it claims to be revealed is "nothing but a bare prejudice."[23]

Hazony believes the entirety of the Hebrew Scriptures is meant to give wisdom that leads to life in God's kingdom. The point of the history of Israel is not simply to give facts about

---

[22] Pennington, *Jesus*, 34.
[23] Yoram Hazony, *The Philosophy of Hebrew Scripture* (Cambridge: Cambridge University Press, 2012), 12.

historical events but to cast a vision of the true and the good for the world. The Hebrew Scriptures are providing a philosophy for all people.[24] It is these scriptures that Jesus studied and explained as he lived and presented a new way of life, God's kingdom on earth as it is in heaven—a redeemed relationship that God has revealed in creation, in the Scriptures, in Jesus, and with the Spirit. Jesus made the Scriptures come to life through his recounting of the Old Testament, further explanations, parables, questions, and stories. Like the philosophers of his day, he used parables and proverbs that got people's attention with an intent for reflection. Consider some of Jesus' parables and proverbs. They reveal the big-picture questions that lead to kingdom-of-heaven life—the good life:

- Give to Caesar what is Caesar's and to God what is God's. (Mark 12:17)
- What does it profit if someone gains the whole world and loses their soul? (Matthew 16:26)
- The last shall be first and the first shall be last. (Matthew 20:16)
- The Sabbath was made for man, not man for the Sabbath. (Mark 2:27)
- Which is lawful on the Sabbath, to do good or to do evil? To save life or destroy it? (Mark 3:4)
- It is impossible to serve two masters, (Matthew 6:24)

---

[24] Pennington, *Jesus*, 51.

- Ask and it will be given, knock and the door will be opened, seek you will find. (Matthew 7:7–8)
- Can the blind lead the blind? (Luke 6:39–40)
- Out of the overflow of the heart mouth speaks. (Luke 6:45)

Getting to the Core

Jesus' teachings addressed the core of people's emotions. Jesus' philosophical, reflective Sermon on the Mount would have been shocking to the ancient world, as he addresses emotions through God-directed meditation.[25] "According to Jesus, the Good is found by looking at God himself, who is *teleios* (whole, mature, complete, perfect Matthew 5:48)."[26] He knows and teaches his way of life (or philosophy) as something crucial and urgent for entering the kingdom of heaven. Jesus calls his hearers/disciples to put into practice what he has said and to do what he has taught based on core beliefs and his philosophy of seeing and being in the world.

Since the pagan Greco-Roman world lived in fear of the emotional unpredictability of the gods, and the anger of these gods was appeased through mysterious rituals, potions, and spells, philosophers sought to offer a way of life that would allow people to find peace.[27] Jesus, as the Master Teacher and greatest prophet, offers hope through viewing the world and the one God through divine revelations that far surpass the world's wisdom. The Master Teacher reasons powerfully as he debates

---

[25] Pennington, *Jesus*, 125.
[26] Pennington, *Jesus*, 66.
[27] Pennington, *Jesus*, 91.

intellectual and religious leaders using practical illustrations. He also teaches that a set of doctrines does not distinguish Christians, but rather love for one another (John 13:34–35). Penington wisely notes, "Christian discipleship changed people's values, sensibilities, hopes, imaginations, habits, and virtues. There is nothing more dangerous and unsettling to society than that."[28]

These are but a few of the reasons that those who follow Jesus must first address matters of their heart and is why teachers who seek to teach Jesus' ways need to address the big-picture questions that begin with our core beliefs and values.

Jesus, the Master Teacher, appealed to the heart. He taught people to think, discerning their belief systems and teaching them to live life from those. He called his followers then and now to evaluate their core values and to change them as needed. He offers hope for change, brought about by living this inside-out life.

Today, we tend to turn the questions we face into objective problems to be fixed. Palmer explains, "That is why we train doctors to repair the body but not honor the spirit; clergy to be CEO's but not spiritual guides; teachers to master techniques but not to engage the student's hearts—or their own."[29]

He continues, describing the need for teachers to model Jesus' appeal to the heart: "Deep speaks to deep, and when we have not sounded our own depths, we cannot sound the depths of our students' lives."[30]

---

[28] Pennington, *Jesus*, 125.
[29] Palmer, "The Heart."
[30] Palmer, "The Heart."

The Big Questions

Jesus asked questions that addressed the big-picture concerns of life. What does it profit if someone gains the whole world but forfeits their soul? (Matthew 16:26). Why do you worry about such things. Can any of you add an hour to your life by worrying? (Matthew 6:27). Do you want to get well? (John 5:6). Who of you is without sin and can cast the first stone? (John 8:7). Why do you call me Lord and not do the things I say? (Luke 6:46) These are deep questions, deep speaking to deep.

Reflective questions can have powerful, life-altering impact, and Jesus was the master of questions. Questions call us to think, allowing them to become transformational, offering renewal to our lives. As learners, humility helps us ask questions. Asking questions shows that we realize we don't know things and that we want to learn from another. As noted earlier, even Jesus, God in the flesh, asked questions of the elders in the temple when he was a boy.

Finding Out Where We Are

When we ask questions, we are forced to stop and think, or pause to consider; to not only consider answers about our inquiries, but to learn about our hearts and discover "where we are." In the first few chapters of Genesis, we often read the words "And God said." In these statements, we learn facts. In Genesis 3:9, we find God's first recorded question. "But the Lord God called to the man, 'Where are you?'" After missing the mark of God's plan, Adam was afraid, recognized his nakedness, and subsequently felt shame. God then posed his second question, "Who told you that you were naked?" In God's first question to Adam, it was not that he did not know where Adam was. Of course he knew. So, why would he ask? Perhaps he asked so that Adam could hear the question and through that question realize where he was—hiding from God, naked and ashamed. From God's question, Adam could also learn that God was seeking him, wanting to restore the relationship. Today, these remain deeply important questions for us to answer: *Where are you? Who told you this?*

Pause to Consider:

- Take a moment to imagine God calling to you, "Where are you?" You might be like Adam, afraid and hiding. If so, consider God's next question: "Who told you this?" What voices tell you that you are not enough and need to hide from God?

Questions demand a response if we take time to consider them. Answering questions helps us discern *where we are.*

Questions Help Us Discern

My friend Gordon Ferguson once made a statement to me that I have not forgotten. Wyndham (my late husband) and I were helping him and Theresa with an issue with their marriage. I felt intimidated to offer any counsel, as I had always looked up to Gordon. Realizing this, he said to me something like, "You know, I have counseled many people about life and marriage, and I even know what I need to hear because of what I know I would say to them. But something unique happens when someone else asks you questions or speaks to you. We need other people to ask us questions." I then realized that teaching is not mainly about me finding the perfect answer or wise saying. It's often in the questions where we help others find the answers. However, too often we don't take time to reflect on questions. Why might this be? To answer this, I will offer some exercises that can help us value questions, hopefully learning to ask them of ourselves and others. But first…

Pause to Consider:

- What holds me back from slowing down to reflect on questions?

Jesus' Questions

Jesus asked questions, lots of them, but answered very few. In Matthew, Jesus asked 109 questions; in Mark, 68 questions; in Luke, 107 questions; in John, 55 questions, and in Acts, he asks Saul one question. Some of Jesus' questions were for inquiry, to find out information. "Who do people say I am?" But even this question led to a personal question. "Who do you say I am?" Jesus asked many types of questions. Some called for soul searching, some seemed designed to challenge current ways of thinking, some were to help people realize where they were, some were to persuade crowds, and some were to offer hope and inspire faith.

I try to imagine hearing Jesus ask, "What good will it be for someone to gain the whole world, yet forfeit their soul?" (Matthew 16:26a.) I believe his question would cause some angst if I were too attached to what this world has to offer. Upon contemplation, I would have to consider ways I might be holding such an attitude without realizing it. This is a reason why questions are so important to teaching. Has any question caused more people to think about their values and shift the trajectory of their lives than the one just mentioned?

Questions Encourage Transformation

Why are questions so powerful for encouraging change? Ponder this a moment. I believe they bring greater clarity concerning our beliefs and motivations. Proverbs 20:5 says, "The purposes of a person's heart are deep waters, but one who has insight draws them out." In a book by Bob Tiede on Jesus' questions, the author notes that questions help us understand what we think, come to know why we think as we do, and discover what deeper purposes motivate us. They also help us build deeper relationships as they invite listening, which brings people together.[31]

Questions can appeal to common ground, which fosters bridge building rather than building walls. We mainly ask questions because we want to know and learn, but there are also

[31] Bob Tiede, 340 *Questions Jesus Asked* (LeadingWithQuestions.com, 2024), https://bob-tiede.s3.us-east-2.amazonaws.com/340_Questions_EBOOK_4–10.pdf.

less-than-humble motives for asking questions. The Pharisees asked questions, but theirs were to trap Jesus or to promote legalism. Their questions sought to build walls and close gates rather than build bridges and understanding. Sincere questions invite us to think, encouraging us to reconsider our core values and deepest commitments that guide the way we live.

Jesus asked thought questions that bring the potential to change our thinking and priorities, such as: "Is not life more than food, and the body more than clothes?" (Matthew 6:25b). "Look at the birds of the air; they do not sow or reap or store away in barns, and yet your heavenly Father feeds them. Are you not much more valuable than they?" (Matthew 6:26). "Can any one of you by worrying add a single hour to your life?" (Matthew 6:27). "Why do you break the command of God for the sake of your tradition?" (Matthew 15:3).

Jesus asked questions of invitation (What are you looking for?), questions concerning his identity (Who do you say I am?), questions about attitudes (Why did you grumble about the splinter in your friend's eye, but not notice the log in your own?), questions about love (Don't even tax collectors love those who love them?), questions about healing (Do you want to get well?), questions about the purpose of life (Is life not about more than food and clothing?), questions about God's kingdom (What shall I compare the kingdom of God to?), questions about faith (Do you believe I can do this?), questions about obedience (Why do you call me "Lord" but don't keep my words?), questions about discipleship (Do you also want to leave?), and questions about eternal life (All who believe in me will never die—do you believe this?)[32] All of these are essential questions for us to meditate on and contemplate. I invite you to take some time to answer these questions, giving your honest answers. Try not to answer with "church answers," or what you would write if someone were to read your journal, but with gut-level honest answers.

Why do you think Jesus asked so many questions? One reason may have been to allow us to make the time and space to answer them. Each time you read one of Jesus' questions, it will be helpful to discern why he may have asked that question. And then, try answering as if he is asking you directly. In many ways, he is.

Jesus' questions were deliberate, and not merely a literary tool to build the narrative of the Gospels. His questions take us straight to significant issues, including those we have previously discussed in this book concerning motivation, identity, and core values. They force us to think and are vital elements contributing toward our spiritual formation, our leadership, our teaching, and our learning. Questions keep us from simply going with the flow, pleasing people, or passively accepting whatever is said or whatever is "on the program," and they help protect us from becoming formulaic in our Christianity. Questions cause us to solve problems we will face and apply our gifts and creativity to life's dilemmas. Often, in the questions, we find answers we were not expecting. Questions remind us that

[32] Bob Tiede, 340 *Questions*

we don't have all the answers, and they remind us of the Spirit's involvement as he continues to guide us into understanding. Questions often uncover things we have previously missed and inspire us with new possibilities.

Asking Hard Questions

Jesus' questions, Job's questions, the psalmist's questions teach us to ask hard questions of God without fear or shame. We can feel freedom to ask where God is amid our deepest suffering, because Jesus demonstrated this angst as he cried, "My God, my God, why have you forsaken me?" (Matthew 27:46; Psalm 22:1).

In Isaiah's prophecy written years before, we get a glimpse of the answer to this heart-wrenching question. The answer lies in the fact that we are in fact, his beloved. Jesus would see the fruit of the anguish of his soul and be satisfied. We, the redeemed, are the fruit of that anguish he felt as he cried out, and amazingly, he believes we were worth it. Wow.

> He will see His offspring,
> He will prolong His days,
> And the good pleasure of the LORD will prosper in His hand.
> As a result of the anguish of His soul,
> He will see it and be satisfied;
> By His knowledge the Righteous One,
> My Servant, will justify the many,
> As He will bear their iniquities. (Isaiah 53:10b–11 NASB1995)

God's love is so deep, universal, and yet personal, that he answered that "why" question with the truest meaning of love. We are God's beloved whom he has always sought to redeem. I invite you to take some time now to consider some questions Jesus asks. These are relational questions, not just fact questions. I invite you to intentionally connect with God's presence, answering as honestly as you can Jesus' questions. You may also want to include some of the questions Jesus asked that were mentioned above.

Pause to Consider:

How do you answer these questions?

- "Who do you say that I am?" (Matthew 16:15b)
- "If you love those who love you, what credit is that to you?" (Luke 6:32) (This powerful question, which Jesus expanded on in the parable of the Good Samaritan, enlarges our duty to love not only our friends, but also our enemies. Has any question encouraged more people to love their neighbors than this one?)
- "Why are you troubled, and why do doubts rise in your minds?" (Luke 24:38)
- When he had finished washing their feet, he put on his clothes and returned to his place. "Do you understand what I have done for you?" he asked them. (John 13:12)
- "What do you want me to do for you?" he asked. (Mark 10:36)
- "What are you looking for?" (John 1:38 NRSV)

Jesus' questions help dispel the distractions that call us away from the big-picture issues. There are many voices, opportunities, and options vying for our attention, yet Jesus' questions can lead us to a fuller understanding of God's love for us. His questions lead us to what is truly important, reaching the core of our deepest beliefs. Experts say there are tens of thousands of pieces of information a day striving to distract us, and Jesus asks the penetrating life-changing questions that pierce the minutia of distractions. The world we live in offers many paths to finding fulfillment: career, money, knowledge, position, power, influence, relationships. These are but some of the "answers" we might be tempted to offer to Jesus' question, "What are you looking for?"

Many people become frustrated when they don't reach the goals they set, but often they don't reach them because they didn't examine or are not even aware of their core values. Jesus' questions point to our core values, making us aware of them so that we can adjust them, learn from him, and find rest for our souls (Matthew 11:28).

Pause to Consider:

Consider the core values/ beliefs behind these questions Jesus asked:

- "Why are you so afraid?" (Matthew 8:26).
- "Why do you look at the speck of sawdust in your brother's eye and pay no attention to the plank in your own eye?" (Matthew 7:3).

- "Why do you entertain evil thoughts in your hearts?" (Matthew 9:4).
- "If a man owns a hundred sheep, and one of them wanders away, will he not leave the ninety-nine on the hills and go to look for the one that wandered off?" (Matthew 18:12).
- "Will not God bring about justice for his chosen ones, who cry out to him day and night?" (Luke 18:7a).

Often, we cannot change the ways we would answer Jesus' questions without first addressing the fundamental beliefs we hold.

Active, Heartfelt Listening

Asking questions brings a crucial aspect of relating to others; that is, a willingness to listen. Active listening is difficult, and Jesus as the Master Teacher was patient and astute in his listening as well as brilliant in his questions.

Have you experienced someone who is supposedly listening but seems far away? Have you been that person? To listen well and learn better from the person we are talking with or teaching, perhaps we should seek to ask questions that draw the person out, that create a safe environment, and that encourage open minds and open hearts. The need to listen is true for all relationships: where we work and lead, with friends and acquaintances, with our spouse and children, with those we know well and those we just met.

Pause to Consider:

- Think of a time you felt heard. What postures and circumstances helped you feel this way?
- What postures, questions, and responses contribute to: drawing someone out? creating a safe environment? nurturing openness? letting another know we care?

By asking questions and listening to responses, we demonstrate that we truly care about another, and we go much deeper in our understanding of them. We connect better, friendships develop, family ties strengthen, trust increases, and love and grace grow. If we did not profoundly matter to Jesus, he would have no desire to ask us questions; he would only give commands. To learn from the Master Teacher, we must take time to answer God's first recorded question: "Where are you?" The Master Teacher seeks to reach our hearts.

In Matthew 19, Jesus has a conversation with a rich young man who asks him a question about what to do to inherit eternal life. Jesus responds with a question. "'Why do you ask me about what is good?' Jesus replied, 'There is only One who is good. If you want to enter life, keep the commandments.'"

Jesus' conversation with this rich young man shows how asking questions can both clarify (getting to the heart of what the word "good" actually means) and expose (the man's concern for wealth). If all good people go to heaven, Jesus presents a dilemma when he states that only God is good. And just as Jesus used a question to clarify and expose, we can do the same thing. How might we use what he did here in a contemporary conversation? Andy Bannister recounts a conversation between a girl named Alice and her classmate concerning moral relativism that both clarifies and exposes:

> Alice's classmate argues, "We don't need God to be good. We just each decide what's right for ourselves, and what's right for you to do may not be right for me to do. The one thing we must never do is tell another person they're wrong." Alice answers, "If there is no God, how do you decide which events are good and which are evil?"
>
> Looking at her classmate's cup on the desk she asked, "Is that your coffee?" "Yes, that's my grande quad nonfat cappuccino." "Brilliant, I love that stuff!" And with that, Alice reached out, grabbed the coffee, and took a large gulp. "What the heck are you doing?" her classmate protested. "Taking your coffee," Alice replied with a grin. "But it's my coffee!" "It was. But you've convinced me that we get to decide good and evil for ourselves, that there's nothing inherently wrong with theft, and so I thought I'd take your coffee. Do you have a problem with that?" "Well...yes." "So would you say it seems to be the case that at least some moral values are bigger than just personal preference?" Suffice it to say, the conversation went in a more productive direction from that point.[33]

[33] Andy Bannister, "Learning Questions from the Master," in Bob Tiede, *340 Questions, 71-72.*

Questions That Breed Humility

Questions help one come to conclusions that they may not have expected. The Quakers are known for a practice using a clearness committee. This committee consists of peers who pose questions and allow the person to come to their own conclusions. This provides an opportunity to listen to oneself.[34] When you are asking a good question, you are adopting a posture of humility. You're confessing that you don't know, and you want to learn. You're also honoring a person.[35] Humble questions are also open ended and show respect. They encourage the other person to take control and take the conversation where they want it to go. These are questions that begin with phrases like, "How did you?" "What's it like?" Will you tell me about?" "In what ways?" "What crossroads are you at?[36] Other questions might include, "What would you do if you weren't afraid?" "If you died tonight, what would you regret not doing?" If we meet a year from now, what will we be celebrating? If the next five years is a chapter in your life, what is that chapter about? Can you be yourself where you are and still fit in? Why is that a problem for you? What's working really well in your life? What are you most self-confident about? Have you ever been alone without feeling lonely? What has become clearer to you as you have aged?"[37] While the goal is not to interrogate, these are just a

[34] Brooks, *How to Know,* 79.
[35] Brooks, *How to Know,* 87.
[36] Brooks, *How to Know,* 88.
[37] Brooks, *How to Know,* 90-91..

few types of questions that let a person know you are interested in their life. Jesus certainly asked questions that helped people become aware of the issues most important to life. Questions can also engage our minds and hearts toward healthy avenues of thought.

Asking a question such as, "What are you thankful for today?" can help someone pause to consider and think of something to be grateful for, which can affect and transform the outlook of their day. Similarly, asking a question like "Who has encouraged you lately?" can also lead toward a more grateful posture, and a question like, "How has God surprised you lately?" can evoke deeper thought concerning God's care and involvement in our lives. When teachers, or any of us, demonstrate a heart of love and integrity through such questions, we help create dialogue that fosters moving forward together, even with our opponents.[38]

Jesus, the Master Teacher, philosopher, question asker, and redeemer, was more than a teacher. His life modeled his teaching, and his sacrificial love showed how deeply he cared. He did not approach his teaching by simply imparting facts to learn or rules to obey. He reached into the deepest recesses of people's hearts to their core values and beliefs, transforming and renewing their hearts to experience life to the full.

[38] Brooks, *How to Know,* 41.

One of my favorite teachers just spent extra time with me, knowing that I was struggling. – Julie

They knew how to connect with their students and make them feel valued. To this day, yes, thirty plus years later, I still keep in touch with them. – Dat

She gave her AP students her phone number and let us call with questions up to 10:00 pm any night! She was so dedicated to us, and no question was ever shamed or belittled. – Karen

She took time to really listen. She would converse with us on a deeper level than any other teacher I had ever had. She was my safe space person. I think I became an educator largely because of her influence on me. – Michelle

She related to us in a way that drew us in…an impressive feat in those notoriously difficult years. We respected her. She was always fair but gave the benefit of the doubt, made us laugh, and kept our attention. When I decided to become a high school teacher, I thought of her often, wanting my students to feel what she made me feel. – Mary Bea

My favorite teachers were the ones who listened and really thought about the needs of those they were teaching. They were the ones from whom I could learn things I didn't know or understand. Then, I was able to grow and change as a person. – Corene

There was something about them that made me feel safe. – Carla

She was inspiring and a safe place, believing in me. I called her late one night when my parents were fighting, and she came and picked me up. My favorite Bible teachers are those with empathetic hearts and a wisdom to keep learning even as they teach. – Kel

Chapter Four

The Master Teacher Sees and Hears

The Samaritan woman, Mary, Nicodemus, the rich young ruler, the woman caught in adultery. Jesus did not see what others saw; he saw *them!* Perhaps our deepest felt need is the need to be seen and heard, to be known. Now that I am a widow, I keenly feel the absence of a witness to my life—someone who always wanted to know what I was thinking, when I would be home, how I was feeling. I have had to wrestle with the knowledge and belief that Jesus witnesses my life, and cares. He could not state it any more clearly than in his words, "Are not two sparrows sold for a penny? Yet not one of them will fall to the ground outside your Father's care. And even the very hairs of your head are all numbered. So don't be afraid; you are worth more than many sparrows" (Matthew 10:29–31). We all must decide whether we believe this to be true for our lives, not just others' lives.

Since I have wrestled with this thought and often spoken with Jesus about my heart, I have noticed more keenly his demonstration of his care. I will share six specific "Jesus really sees me" experiences that I have had since becoming a widow. I have named the experiences the phone call, the goose, the eagle, the wedding, the paper clip, and the dog. I share these stories as a testimony and reminder that when we wrestle relationally with Jesus and expect him to show up via the Spirit, we will more clearly see him at work.

Feeling Seen and Heard

About a year after Wyndham died, I was plagued with thoughts of not knowing what paradise was like and whether Wyndham was aware of things on earth, including me. I wanted him to know about the pandemic; about changes in his favorite sports teams; about my retiring; about some grandkids getting baptized; about me finishing my book, moving, and getting my doctorate; and so much more. As a deeply godly man, he is certainly with Jesus, but I longed to know more what that looks like. In a very tearful prayer one morning, I begged God to help me understand. I kept repeating the phrase in my prayer, "More than anything, I just want to know he is okay." I cried hard for a while, repeating this phrase. Then the phone rang. It was a call from a woman I did not know well, but had briefly met perhaps one or two times. She was from another region of my church. Her message was simply this: "Hi, this is Kathy. You may not remember me, and I feel really strange calling with this message, but something told me that I needed to call you and let you know that 'everything is okay.'" That's all she said, but she said she felt compelled to call me to deliver this message. I still get chills thinking about this. Thank you, God, for seeing and hearing me.

Then, there was the goose. When I moved to Connecticut,

I began walking a trail alongside the nearby river, a beautifully landscaped three-mile walk. I feel a special connection with geese, and wrote about this connection because of a goose that resided at my parents' home and "adopted" each of them before they passed. I told this story, entitled "Understanding Goose," in my book about adoption issues. As soon as I arrived in Connecticut and began walking this trail, an unusual phenomenon caught the attention of people down at the river. Seemingly the day I arrived, a lone goose took residence at the dock by the boathouse, and it stayed there for months. It was all alone. The phenomenon about geese that resonated with me was the fact that they have a mate for life. When they lose a mate, if given the chance, they attach to a person as if that person were their new mate. I have at times felt that when I see a "lone goose," it is a small reminder or hug from God that he remembers and thinks of me. The goose stayed for several months as I adjusted to my new move, a new house, new surroundings, and life without my husband. One day, about three months later, it disappeared as suddenly as it had appeared. I reasoned with Jesus that perhaps it was time for me to fully adjust and spread my wings. I told him that now that the goose was gone, it would be encouraging to see an eagle as a reminder that I was ready to soar. I am not kidding when I tell you that as I was having this conversation, an eagle crossed the river and flew directly over my head. I have not seen anything like this before or since.

The next "seen and heard" moment came when I was thinking, for some reason (I cannot remember who it was), about someone's wedding. I told God that I would have loved to perform a wedding, as they are such joyous occasions. But then I laughed, telling him that I could not imagine any kind of scenario where that might happen. And yes, you may have guessed as you read this. A few weeks after that conversation with God, a woman I had not spoken with for several years, but whom I had once helped navigate through a difficult time in her life, called to ask me to officiate her wedding. Not only was this a great joy for me (and I believe for the couple as well), but God worked through this situation in some amazing, even shocking ways. I felt deeply seen and heard.

The next example, the paper clip, might seem a silly happening, but to me it was another reminder of the joy that comes from being seen and heard. I had been traveling to speak at a conference. Before I left, I had told myself to grab a paper clip, as I did not want my printed notes to get out of order as I spoke, which seems to easily happen to me. I have slight dyslexia, and sometimes numbering and ordering can be problematic. As I walked out of my hotel room to teach my lesson, I realized I had forgotten to bring a paper clip, and it troubled me. I told myself that this was not a big deal and pressed the elevator button to go to the auditorium. As I prepared to get on the elevator, I looked down to find one shiny paper clip. I had to smile and thank Jesus for hearing and seeing me through big and little things.

As I write this chapter, I am enjoying another "seen and heard" moment. At my feet lies Tessie, my new furry friend. I had been pondering a decision to get another dog, as my beloved golden retriever companion, Denver, nears his thirteenth birthday. I have wanted him to help train and influence another dog but was not sure I wanted to get a puppy. In fact, I was pretty sure I did not want a puppy. I reasoned that I would like a two-year-old dog, preferably a rescue, but I also wanted a particular breed. My top choice was a Portuguese water dog. Last month, Denver had an allergy episode that made him itch. I called my vet to make an appointment for him to get his allergy shot. The vet gave me an appointment for the next day, but I asked if there was any way I could come right then. When I received an affirmative reply, I headed over. One other person was there, preparing to pick up his dog, who had sprained her leg. He was conversing with the vet about his regrettable need to rehome his dog, as the man, now in his eighties, had developed severe back pain, needed surgery, and could no longer give his dog what she needed.

I quickly interjected, asking, "How old is your dog?" He replied, "Two years old." I then asked, "What kind of dog is she?" His reply made me laugh inside, but didn't really surprise me. "She's a Portuguese water dog." I am grateful that Jesus, who knows the number of hairs on my head, sees and hears my thoughts and desires. I have become more expectant for Jesus to show up, and he has not disappointed.

I will add that these moments came after five very hard years of caring for Wyndham as I watched multiple system atrophy take over his entire body, leaving him without the ability to move, talk, and finally breathe. During many of these days,

I wondered where God was and why he wasn't answering my prayers as I wished, relating more to Jesus' question, "My God, why have you forsaken me?" Life is not all phone calls, geese, eagles, weddings, paper clips, and pups, but I assure you that God sees and hears. Jesus is a witness to our lives, and he cares. Deeply.

Pause to Consider:

- When were some moments in your life you have felt seen and heard by another person? What did that feel like?
- When were some moments you felt seen and heard by Jesus?
- When were some moments you have been filled with awe at the wonders of God?

Meanings Beyond the Questions

Jesus knew people and spoke to them in ways that have even deeper meaning for us when we become more culturally informed about Ancient Middle Eastern living. When Jesus asked in John 4:35, "Don't you have a saying, 'It's still four months until harvest?'" it meant more to them than it does to us today. We don't have that saying.

When I read Jesus' question about the unmerciful servant in Luke 17:7–10, I again realize the difference in our cultural contexts. Here, Jesus asks a series of questions:

> "Suppose one of you has a servant plowing or looking after the sheep. Will he say to the servant when he comes in from the field, 'Come along now and sit down to eat'? Won't he rather say, 'Prepare my supper, get yourself ready and wait on me while I eat and drink; after that you may eat and drink'? Will he thank the servant because he did what he was told to do? So you also, when you have done everything you were told to do, should say, 'We are unworthy servants; we have only done our duty.'"

In my context, I would answer Jesus' first question with a resounding, "Yes, most certainly I would have him come sit down to eat. This is what you taught me about the last being first, loving my neighbor, and treating others as I want to be treated. And of course I would thank him, but Jesus, I would not even have a servant." From the Ancient Middle Eastern vantage point and way of life, this discourse would have been understood much differently from the ways I view it. Jesus helped those he was teaching understand forgiveness, faith, and duty from the context in which they functioned. I view it from the vantage point that entitlement must go away when we understand what Jesus teaches.

In John 4, Jesus saw and heard the woman at the well and began a conversation with her. They discussed her understanding of worship. I don't think she was changing the subject when speaking about where Jews worship; her comments actually showed her knowledge of culturally appropriate worship. We also don't know the why's of the situation of her numerous husbands. Perhaps she had been widowed five times or had been divorced. We also don't know how she ended up being with a man who was not her husband. She may have been purchased as a concubine. Or maybe she was living in an immoral relationship by choice. We don't know, but we see Jesus address her current understanding of separate worship for her and the Israelites. Then, Jesus explains that Jews and Gentiles will worship together in spirit and truth, no matter the place. His answer is not really about worship location, as he teaches something much more profound: that Jews and Gentiles—all people—can worship together in Spirit and truth. In response, the woman convinced many to believe in Jesus. This shows she must have been a trusted woman of influence that people would take seriously.

In Matthew 11:16–17, Jesus asks, "To what can I compare this generation? They are like children sitting in the marketplaces and calling out to others: 'We played the pipe for you, and you did not dance; we sang a dirge, and you did not mourn.'" I am not familiar with dancing to pipes or mourning with dirges, but Jesus' audience was. He used the customs and cultures of the people to make important points. He saw and heard people according to what they needed and within their context, and there were times when he had different responses to similar situations.

Jesus Related to All Different Kinds of People

John includes descriptions of Jesus teaching many different types of people, such as the respected Pharisee Nicodemus and the Samaritan woman, who would have been considered a half-breed. We often ascribe to her a moral lack, though as previously mentioned, this is an assumption. Jesus purposely had conversations with people of different ethnicities, genders, and societal standings in his early ministry in Judea, teaching and sharing some of his best-known promises using stories and parables that include these different groups. In Matthew 9:10, as sinners and tax collectors sit down with Jesus, he teaches the importance of table fellowship. He then told the murmurers, while quoting Hoseas 6:6, to go and learn what this means: "I desire mercy, not sacrifice." He didn't tell them facts, he asked them to "pause to consider," knowing they needed introspection and ability to see those around them with love.

Pause to Consider:

- Using this example where Jesus quotes Hosea 6:6, can you think of situations when Jesus might say to you, "Consider what this means: I desire mercy, not sacrifice?"

Jesus Emoted

Jesus can see and hear us well because he experienced the full gamut of human emotions. He wept, marveled, hoped, and longed for certain things to happen; he lamented (Matthew 8:10, 27:46; Luke 19:41; Hebrews 12:2). The three emotions of Jesus described most frequently are compassion, anger (at compassionless people), and joy. He rejoices regularly, giving thanks joyfully in all circumstances and instructing his disciples to do the same (Luke 10:21; John 15:11, 17:13). Compassion, sorrow, and indignation are rightly joined together. B. B. Warfield aptly states, "Joy and sorrow meet in his heart and kiss each other."[39] "His emotions never master him or function wrongly."[40]

Truly he was tempted in all ways like we are, yet was without sin (Hebrews 4:15). Emotions are God-given gifts, and only when we let them overtake godliness are they destructive.

The Master Teacher Understands

Nobody could see and understand people like Jesus could. He could read human hearts (John 2:25), though he did not control them. Was that a divine, supernatural ability, or was it the result of such compassion that he paid attention? While we don't know for sure, he saw in those ordinary men and women whom he called to follow him something extraordinary. He saw in an unnamed woman a depth of gratitude so large she would be remembered forever (Matthew 26:6–13). He saw in Saul, the terrorist, someone who could, with his education, languages, and background, reach a demographic no one else could. As I heard one scholar say, Paul was so uniquely qualified for his role that if he didn't exist, he would have to be invented.[41] Jesus

---

[39] B. B. Warfield, "On the Emotional Side of Our Lord," in The Person and Work of Christ (Phillipsburg, NJ: P&R, 1989), 141.

[40] Warfield, "On the Emotional," 111.

[41] From a conversation with Mark Wilson, Pauline scholar, June 22, 2024.

saw in a tax collector someone who needed a face-to-face lunch meeting to come to faith and repentance. He saw in Thomas one who needed to touch the wounds in his hands and side. He saw in Mary and Martha their need for comfort and empathy. He saw. He heard. He knew how to connect, and today's world desperately needs to learn from the Master Teacher how to see others, connect with them, and love them.

The Price of Disconnection

Many people, even in families, have not learned to see and hear each other, so they lack needed connection. This disconnect carries sad, frightening consequences. Between 1999 and 2019, American suicide rates increased by 33 percent. Between 2009 and 2019, the percentage of teens who reported "persistent feelings of sadness or hopelessness" rose from 26 percent to 37 percent. By 2021, it had shot up to 44 percent. The percentage of Americans who said they have no close friends quadrupled between 1990 and 2020. In one survey, 54 percent of Americans reported that no one knows them well. And 36 percent of Americans reported that they felt lonely frequently or almost all the time, including 61 percent of young adults and 51 percent of young mothers.[42]

When people feel unseen, they tend to shut down relationally and socially. People who are lonely and unseen can easily become suspicious, taking offense when none is intended. They

[42] Brooks, *How to Know*, 98.

become afraid of the very thing they need most, which is intimate contact with other humans. Because they feel unworthy of people's attention, having been starved for it, they tend to be filled with self-loathing and self-doubt. As Brooks notes, it feels shameful to think you are unworthy of other people's attention.[43] Jesus knows when we feel shame, and like God did with Adam, can provide clothes from sacrifice to cover our shame. He saw Adam, and he sees us. Because he sees and hears so well, he is the Master Teacher.

Pause to Consider:

- Is there a time when you have felt unseen? How did you respond? What difference might it make if you really believe Jesus sees you and cares for you?

The Importance of Being Seen

In *The Body Keeps the Score,* author Bessel van der Kolk writes, "Knowing that we are seen and heard by the important people in our lives can make us feel calm and safe, and… being ignored or dismissed can precipitate rage reactions or mental collapse."[44] Sadness, lack of recognition, and loneliness turn into bitterness. Brooks's many conversations on this topic reveal that when people believe their identity is insignificant and doesn't matter, it feels like injustice…because it is. People

---

[43] Brooks, *How to Know,* 99.

[44] Bessel van der Kolk, *The Body Keeps the Score: Brain, Mind, and Body in the Healing of Trauma* (London: Penguin Books, 2015), 80, cited in Brooks, *How to Know,* 100.

who have been treated unjustly often lash out, seeking ways to humiliate those they feel have humiliated them. As the saying goes, hurt people hurt people. Loneliness thus leads to meanness. As another saying goes, pain that is not transformed gets transmitted. People become proud of their bitterness in this social breakdown.[45] Jesus' care and compassion for us can become the transforming agent that turns bitterness into forgiveness, isolation into welcoming, rejection into acceptance, and sadness into joy.

Brooks continues, pointing out that one of people's greatest needs is to have another person look into their face with loving respect and acceptance.[46] How perfectly Jesus models this: "Jesus looked at him and loved him" (Mark 10:21). "Woman, why are you crying?" (John 20:13). "Bring the boy here to me" (Matthew 17:17). He took the children in his arms and blessed them (Mark 10:16). He looks at and he loves rather than looks at and judges (think of the rich young ruler and the woman caught in adultery). His judgment is directed toward the judgers, not the sinners.

Jesus' teaching flowed from the ways he saw and heard, with eyes and ears of love. He saw people in ways that others did not, as told in the parable about the man who had been robbed, the story we know as The Good Samaritan (Luke 10:29–37). He saw the true neighbor as the marginalized outlier. He saw and heard rulers such as Nicodemus and the other Pharisees

[45] Brooks, *How to Know,* 100.

[46] Brooks, *How to Know,* 8.

as clearly as he saw men and women who were considered nobodies and low-down sinners. He saw individuals, and he saw crowds. Sometimes, we can mistakenly think that teaching demands a crowd, but I find that the most meaningful teaching situations often go unnoticed, taking place with those whom some would see as undeserving.

Jesus notices hearts seeking him. He told Nathanael, *"I saw you…*under the fig tree." Repeatedly, Jesus sees people not as projects, but as people to love. He heard them. Jesus listened to people and their questions, asking them questions as well. He listened for what the deeper issues were, often reminding them of what they said they believed.

He reacted differently according to what people needed. Matthew 12:3–4 recounts, "Haven't you read what David did when he and his companions were hungry? He entered the house of God, and he and his companions ate the consecrated bread—which was not lawful for them to do, but only for the priests." At other times, people were punished for disobedience like this. Jesus addressed what was in the heart, even trumping earlier-created laws.

Seeing with Love

Jesus' gaze communicated. Somehow, it was evident in his encounter with the rich young ruler that he looked at him and loved him (Mark 10:21). The children were not afraid to come to Jesus (Mark 10:13–16). The bleeding woman sought to touch the hem of his garment (Luke 8:43–48). Jesus' gaze at Peter, after Peter had denied him, brought Peter deep remorse (Luke

22:61–62). Tenderness communicates deep emotional concern about another being, and this was evident with Jesus. Jesus, the Son of God who spoke with all authority, is described as gentle (Matthew 11:29). Learning from him, we can learn to see and hear with gentleness, a fruit of the Spirit, as we teach.

Often, our inability to see and hear stems from preoccupation with our own selves. Our ability to see others means overcoming insecurities and self-focus, opening ourselves up to the experience of another. In describing how to better see people, Brooks shares the importance of putting ourselves in another's shoes, with curiosity about their life. He shares novelist Zadie Smith's words that helped her write compelling stories: "I wanted to know what it was like to be everybody. I wondered what it would be like to believe the sorts of things I didn't believe." Brooks adds, "What a fantastic way to train our imagination in the art of seeing others."[47] When we are not strong in seeing through another's eyes, we need help learning to do so. Perhaps this is a reason Jesus used so many stories and parables: to help us see others' lives outside our frame of reference, peering into their life situations and emotions.

Pause to Consider:

- Think of a time you felt seen with tenderness. What were the circumstances, and how did that affect you?
- What might you do to train your imagination in the art of seeing others better?

---

[47] Brooks, *How to Know*, 34.

Reaching to the Heart

As products of the Enlightenment, our Western culture separates reason from emotion. Jesus combines the two, as his teaching poignantly addresses the heart. As Jesus taught from the story "The Good Samaritan," he describes the godly, neighborly response from the one who entered into the injured man's experience and did something to help him. The failures of others weren't intellectual failures, but failures of the heart. Iris Murdoch wisely states:

> The essential immoral act is the inability to see others correctly. Humans tend to be self-centered, anxious, and resentful. We are constantly representing people to ourselves in self-serving ways, in ways that gratify our egos and serve our ends, thus [we] stereotype and condescend, ignore and dehumanize. The essential moral act is to cast a "just and loving attention."[48]

Jesus exemplifies this just and loving attention, seeing correctly from his humble, servant heart.

Jesus' Posture

Jesus' attention to those he taught can be seen not only through his gaze, but also in his posture. It seems notable that when Jesus quoted Scripture he was usually, if not always, standing. When he taught crowds, he often sat down. While

[48] Iris Murdoch, *The Sovereignty of Good* (Abingdon, UK: Routledge, 2014), 36.

this was culturally appropriate, perhaps there are lessons we might learn from his postures.

> In that hour Jesus said to the crowd, "Am I leading a rebellion, that you have come out with swords and clubs to capture me? Every day I sat in the temple courts teaching, and you did not arrest me." (Matthew 26:55)

> Again Jesus began to teach by the lake. The crowd that gathered around him was so large that he got into a boat and sat in it out on the lake, while all the people were along the shore at the water's edge. (Mark 4:1)

> At dawn he appeared again in the temple courts, where all the people gathered around him, and he sat down to teach them. (John 8:2)

I can feel the drama intensify in this passage as Jesus begins his teaching ministry:

> He went to Nazareth, where he had been brought up, and on the Sabbath day he went into the synagogue, as was his custom. He stood up to read, and the scroll of the prophet Isaiah was handed to him. Unrolling it, he found the place where it is written:
>
> "The Spirit of the Lord is on me,
> because he has anointed me

> to proclaim good news to the poor.
> He has sent me to proclaim freedom for the prisoners
> and recovery of sight for the blind,
> to set the oppressed free,
> to proclaim the year of the Lord's favor."
>
> Then he rolled up the scroll, gave it back to the attendant and sat down. The eyes of everyone in the synagogue were fastened on him. He began by saying to them, "Today this scripture is fulfilled in your hearing." (Luke 4:16–21)

Of note, at least to me, is the respect Jesus gives the Scriptures as he unrolls the scroll, stands up to read, and after he reads, sits down. I have been in several settings where, when Scripture is read, the speaker states, "The word of the Lord," and the congregation in unison replies, "The word of the Lord." Though I imagine it can easily become rote habit, I believe it can also have significant meaning when showing respect for God's word.

I wonder what would happen if our teaching involved standing when the Scriptures are read, and then the teacher or preacher sitting down as they teach or preach. The rise of evangelicalism puts the preacher and pulpit front and center, often elevated. This seems quite different from Jesus' posture of sitting to teach. It seems more congruent with many of the configurations that involved "doing church" from the earliest of days. Thoughts to consider.

The Teacher's Timing and Use of Stories

As I close my eyes to imagine a scene in Nazareth, I try to involve my senses. On this day, the usual sounds and smells of the marketplace are suspended, for it is the Sabbath. I watch Jesus enter the local synagogue, which is no surprise, since this is his Sabbath custom. But as I peer inside, this day, something extraordinary happens. He stands up, someone hands him a scroll, and he begins unrolling it. His finger searches the parchment and then comes to rest.

What happens next seems a blur. What is this teacher saying? And why? His next words answer the why. It's time. Time to teach. He is sent to proclaim freedom for the oppressed and to proclaim the year of the Lord's favor. And that favor is now with Jesus, God in the flesh, as Jesus begins teaching about a kingdom of heaven. God's Spirit is on him, and as he reads, the Spirit's presence is evident to behold. The silence following Jesus' reading and proclamation sounds deafening as he rolls up the scroll, looks at the people, and says, "Today this scripture is fulfilled in your hearing." I would have to know something of great significance just happened.

Jesus always had a sense of timing. The beginning of his ministry was marked by this particular time and place, but his preparation had been lifelong. It was no accident that after his baptism he went into the wilderness for time alone with God, where he was tempted. In the Bible, wilderness sojourns and temptations seem to always precede ministry or teaching preparation. Too seldom in our time do teaching ministries and preaching begin after a time of preparation and testing. As the saying goes, the only way to get five years of experience is with five years of experience.

Pause to Consider:

- What "wilderness journeys" in your life have helped to prepare you for your own ministry as a follower of Jesus? How important was (is) this time to your faith, understanding, and relatability?

Jesus would fulfill scriptures that were spoken by the prophets many years prior, and he would finally defeat the power of the evil one by overcoming the final enemy, death. Luke 4, quoted previously and repeated from Isaiah, is just one example of fulfilled prophesy. While many prophecies about Jesus are found in Isaiah, Isaiah 40 describes the Great Shepherd. This prophecy was fulfilled when God incarnate came as the Good Shepherd to give his life for the sheep, search for the lost sheep, and bring back the strays. The timing of prophetic fulfillment, along with the political and cultural environments, all came together for the exact timing of Jesus' arrival and ministry. God's timing is not always understood, for sure, but it is not accidental.

Waiting Is Hard

We are a people who don't like to wait. Jesus' teaching followed times of wilderness, fasting, praying, and long nights. He had a season of withdrawal before his last journey to Jerusalem and the cross (Jn 12:36). Matthew 15 speaks of his withdrawal to the surrounding Gentile regions. Jesus took time to make needed transitions. Mark 3:13–14 tells us of one of those days, when Jesus spent all night in prayer on the mountain. He then called his disciples to him and chose twelve.

Jesus had a sense of timing but could also be persuaded to change it, as noted when he responded to his mother's request by performing his first recorded miracle, turning water into wine (Jn 2:4). I imagine Mary had seen Jesus do miracles before asking him to do one at the wedding feast. Many times, he asked those he healed to keep his identity to themselves, due to it not being the best time for such recognition. This seldom worked, as people could not hold in their good news. So even Jesus' plans did not always go as he wished. This gives me much hope, knowing he could both relate to plans gone awry and trust that the "new plans" could still be used to God's glory.

Jesus was aware of people's human limitations, as demonstrated in his feeding of the 5,000 and 4,000. He felt compassion for the people who had remained with him for three days and had nothing to eat. He read the room, noticing their tiredness and hunger and saying, "If I send them home hungry, they will collapse on the way, because some of them have come a long distance" (Mk 8:3). Jesus was busy teaching, but his compassion moved him to feed them, aware of the time.

Pause to Consider:

- What is your practice of waiting and prayer in

preparation for teaching or learning?
- How has the Holy Spirit directed your sense of timing?

Timing and Trust

Sometimes people aren't ready to be taught. Jesus was aware of this, but also knew that love brought the best timing. As a popular book title notes, there is a "speed of trust." Jesus accompanied his disciples, and they accompanied him. They learned to trust him, as he was always worthy of it. It took time to build trust. I am grateful that Jesus recognizes that trust takes time. Previously mentioned, but worthy of repetition, is that John records the time when Thomas doubts and asks to touch Jesus' wounds for confirmation of his resurrection, to which Jesus replies, "Because you have seen me, you have believed; blessed are those who have not seen and yet have believed" (John 20:29). I really appreciate Jesus' awareness and acknowledgment, because it is harder to trust without physical presence. Jesus sees and hears this. It takes time.

Accompaniment is a necessary stage in getting to know a person because it is gentle and measured.[49] D. H. Lawrence states this well:

> Whoever wants life must go softly toward life, softly as one would go towards a deer and fawn that are nestling under a tree. One gesture of violence, one violent assertion of self-will and life is gone.... But with quietness, with an abandon of self-assertion and a fullness

[49] Brooks, *How to Know,* 47.

> of deep true self one can approach another human being, and know the delicate best of life, the touch.[50]

When my husband and I adopted our youngest son at the age of twelve, a wise psychologist told us something I did not wish to hear at the time. She said it takes children who have been abandoned in orphanages as many years to learn to trust as the number of years they were not in your family. Unfortunately, I found this to be all too true. It took more time than I would have imagined to build trust, and the consistency of our unconditional love was necessary. Thankfully, Jesus gives unconditional love perfectly, and when human hurts have weakened our trust, Jesus will always prove trustworthy. Though Thomas had been with Jesus and saw the resurrected Lord, it still took time for him to trust. And how did Jesus answer his doubt? He let him touch his wounds. We gain trust when we realize that Jesus has experienced pain, rejection, and betrayal like we have, and patiently allows us to metaphorically touch his wounds.

Pause to Consider:

- What are some ways that accompaniment has guided you in your learning or teaching? How might you intentionally better the ways you accompany someone on their journey?

---

[50] D. H. Lawrence, *Lady Chatterley's Lover* (NY: Penguin Books, 2006), 323, cited in Brooks, How to Know, 47.

Can I Get a Witness?

Brooks describes how in normal life, when you accompany someone, you sign on to their plans. In music, the accompanist is sensitive to what the singer is doing and gets a feel for the experience she or he is trying to create.[51] Trust is built when individual differences are appreciated, when mistakes are tolerated, and when one person says, more with facial expression than anything else, "I'll be there when you want me. When the time is right." Accompaniment often involves a surrender of power that is beautiful to behold. Pope Paul VI said, "Modern man listens more willingly to witnesses than teachers, and if he listens to teachers, it's because they are witnesses."[52] God waits for us longingly with open, welcoming arms just as in the Parable of the Prodigal Son the father waits for the son. But he did not keep the son from wandering. God's love allows that same freedom, though he longs to hold the beloved close.

In the Gospels, Jesus lets his followers know that his attention is such that he is aware of the number of hairs on our head and when a sparrow falls to the ground. He assures us we are more valuable than the sparrow (Matthew 10:26–31). I imagine that this kind of attention is possible because God is beyond my comprehension, but also because his divinity has been imparted to me as a partaker of the divine nature (2 Peter 1:4 ESV) so that somehow that "residing divinity" keeps up with and accompanies me.

---

[51] Brooks, *How to Know,* 50.

[52] Brooks, *How to Know,* 52.

The message of Jesus was simple and was repeated many times through different literary tools such as questions and parables. He loves us and longs for a relationship with us. He sees and hears us. He had a perfect sense of timing, and his use of spaced repetition is especially evident in his teachings on love and the heart of the kingdom of God. His repeated message was clear. Through his posture and his gaze, he sees us and hears us, because he loves us. Love does that. It sees and hears. It is a witness to our life. It learns to trust.

My professor assigned a project. Part of the process was to bring my ideas for the project to the class for input. My classmates helped shape the direction I would go with some of my content, and how it would be delivered. We spent a good hour of class time, and the feedback from a diverse community of classmates was priceless. – Jim

I was always grateful for classmates who were not afraid to put up their hand and ask for a repeat of instructions, or ask the "uncomfortable" questions. Often the answer to these questions was the difference between feeling completely lost and having a clear direction or understanding of the subject at hand. – Britain

My high school journalism teacher was also in charge of the school newspaper. I remember the comradery of sharing stories, rooting for each other, gathering ads, and reading others' writings for input. It made me a better writer and caused me to want to be a writer and major in journalism. – SWS

I took an African-American history class in the early 80s at Florida State. I was the only white girl there, and I learned so much in class discussions from my classmates, especially about the color caste systems within their culture that I had no clue about, as well as many other things about their personal experiences. I think any class that allows for personal discussions is enlightening and impacting. – Robin

My middle school (junior high) Sunday school teacher had us paint, arrange the desks and chairs, and decorate the whole classroom. It felt like it was then "ours." I heard she got in trouble for doing that, but I will never forget the comradery built from that joint venture. – Jean

My ninth-grade teacher had recently moved to the US and had a heavy accent. He had trouble giving explanations because of the language barrier, so would repeat himself. He apologized when the students had a bad first quarter and asked for feedback. He began asking students who understood to go to the board and show the class. Once they explained, we all caught on faster, and he learned more English. He showed us that humility can produce solutions and success. – Laura

Community discussion has helped me to learn about different perspectives based on age, race/ethnicity, and spiritual background or experience. It has also helped me slow down and give the time to search my heart for deeper insights about myself and God. – Ayesha

Chapter Five

The Master Teacher and Community

Jesus was the master at building community. When he wasn't with other people, he would be found spending time with the Father in prayer. He knew that the only way the world would see the kingdom of heaven on earth was through the disciples' love for each other (John 13:35). He gathered a diverse group to accompany him, so they could learn together from him and each other. We learn, throughout the Gospels, various ways the disciples' unique backgrounds exposed how they needed to learn from one another. Jesus' teaching employed the practice of community discussion. This can be seen as deliberate and essential as we follow him with his disciples on his teaching journey.

One of Jesus' best-known parables, recorded in Matthew 13, we know as the Parable of the Sower, or the Parable of the Soils. Matthew 13:1–23, Mark 4:1–20, and Luke 8:4–15 all record this teaching. In this parable, Jesus describes four different types of soil (four conditions of the human heart) as a farmer scatters seed (the word of God) on the soil. After teaching this parable, the disciples needed a debriefing. Jesus had gone inside after teaching, and the disciples followed him, wanting explanations. Jesus explained the parable to them and then told them another parable, and yet another, and then one more. All were to help them understand the kingdom of heaven. After the fourth parable, he asked them, "Have you understood all these things?" When they answered affirmatively, he replied, "Therefore every scribe who has been trained for the kingdom of heaven is like a master of a house, who brings out of his treasure what is new and what is old" (Matthew 13:52 ESV). Here, it seems Jesus emphasizes that he is training them to be teachers and scribes, trained for the kingdom of heaven, able to connect the dots of the Old Testament narrative with the fulfillment of God's redemptive plan through Jesus.

In Mark's account of the interaction, he includes, "With many such parables he spoke the word to them, as they were able to hear it. He did not speak to them without a parable, but privately to his own disciples he explained everything" (Mark 4:33–34 ESV). This sheds light on the fact that Jesus' discussions with the group were ever-illuminating, continual, and expected. Without this interaction, they would lack understanding.

If there had been no debriefing within the community, no questions asked, no explanations given, we may never have had any account of the meaning of the parables, as the disciples would not have understood. They would never have become scribes or teachers, because they would have lacked the understanding to connect the story of God's loving redemption begun in the Law and the Prophets and fulfilled in Jesus.

Later, in Matthew 15, Jesus calls a crowd to him, telling them to listen and understand that it is not what goes into a person that defiles them but what comes out of their mouth (Matthew 15:10–11). The disciples think they are letting Jesus in on something when they tell him that the Pharisees were offended, as if Jesus didn't know. Peter makes it clear that the disciples with Jesus have no idea, really, what Jesus is talking about. (Thank you, Peter, for raising your hand to ask the questions others want to know.) I find humor as Jesus, offering further explanation to his disciples asks, "Are you still so dull?" With the closeness he shares with the group, I can't help but wonder if this sounded more like friendly banter.

Then, in Matthew 16, when Jesus warns of the yeast of the Pharisees and Sadducees, he pulls together his disciples' discussion group to let them know he was not talking about yeast used in bread, as they were thinking, but instead the yeast of the harmful teaching of the Pharisees and Sadducees. I think Jesus received the answer to his earlier rhetorical question, "Are you still so dull?" The answer would be "Yes, it certainly seems that way. The guys are over here discussing whether to use Fleischmann's dry yeast, quick-rising, or paste." I don't suppose the disciples forgot that misunderstanding again, and remembered it often when they ate bread. I can imagine during one of their meals one of them bursting out in laughter, remembering when they misunderstood Jesus' teaching in such a big way.

I'll never forget my first year working for HOPE *worldwide*[53] when the CEO was sharing about a fundraising event

[53] Hope *worldwide* is a non-profit international charitable organization.

that was "a dog and pony show." Immediately, I started envisioning the best literal dog and pony show imaginable, only to find out that the phrase was an expression meaning a "grand event." You can only imagine the curious looks I got when I described what I envisioned as a literal dog and pony show, featuring my favorite animals. I must say, in my imagination, it was quite a spectacular show! With this mental lapse in mind, I can imagine Matthew and Philip smirking as they broke bread together, saying, "Dude, you remember when you thought the yeast of the Pharisees was a brand of bread yeast?" "Yeah, cool, bruh." At least I am in good company as I share this embarrassing, "dull" remark.

In Matthew 18, Jesus engaged them in community discussion about who is greatest in the kingdom of heaven, as it seems several were hoping to hear their names mentioned. Imagine their surprise—again, never to be forgotten—when Jesus called a youngster over and told them they needed to become like a little child.

We also read of times when Jesus takes the Twelve aside to teach them what would soon happen to him. In Matthew 20, when James and John's mother wanted special privileges for her boys, the others were indignant. It seems, since the group was upset with James and John, that the boys had likely put "mommy" up to this request. Jesus called the group together and taught them about the first becoming last. Another example of Jesus' many teachings in community comes when Jesus is anointed by the woman at Bethany. Jesus knew the disciples needed a community discussion, as they were so practical about the cost of the ointment that they missed the heart of gratitude and love. They missed the point. Without discussion, we may have never known the meaning of this beautiful act.

Pause to Consider:

- How might the Bible read differently if Jesus had not pulled the disciples together for community discussion?
- Think of a time when discussing Scripture with others changed or enhanced your understanding of the message of Jesus. What were the circumstances that allowed this to happen?
- How might you incorporate more discussion concerning the meaning of Scripture into your learning and teaching?

Our Disconnected Society

Journalist and author David Brooks, in his book *How to Know a Person,* discusses ways we can better learn how to know each other. He describes the context of our world today:

> We meet each other in the current atmosphere of disconnection and distrust. We meet each other as members of groups. We meet each other embodied in systems of power in which some groups have more and some less. Our encounters are shaped by our historical

> inheritances, the legacies of slavery, elitism, sexism, prejudice, bigotry, and social and economic domination. You can't get to know another person while pretending not to see ideology, class, race, faith, identity, or any of the other fraught social categories.[54]

This description of life today was also relevant during Jesus' days on earth. Human nature carries on from generation to generation with the same patterns of disconnection and domination. In Jesus' day, political powers sought to dominate and control. The religious leaders cast judgment on Jesus and his followers and sought to subdue them, attempting to legislate righteousness. They looked down on any who challenged their traditions, staying eager and diligent to maintain the status quo. Ethnic prejudice, favoritism, entitlement, enslavement, and misogyny reigned. This was the landscape for Jesus' teaching then, and remains the backdrop for his teaching today.

Social Breakdown of Connection

Brooks further notes:

> In 2018, the Pew Research Center asked Americans what gave them meaning in life. Only 7 percent said helping other people. Only 11 percent said learning was a source of meaning in their life. The breakdown in moral skills produced disconnection, alienation,

[54] Brooks, *How to Know,* 109.

> and a culture in which cruelty was permitted. Our failure to treat each other well in the small encounters of everyday life metastasized and led to the horrific social breakdown we see all around us.[55]

It is in this atmosphere, and in the immediate context of his impending betrayal, that Jesus instructs, "A new command I give you: Love one another. As I have loved you, so you must love one another. By this everyone will know that you are my disciples, if you love one another" (John 13:34–35 ESV). God, Jesus, and the Spirit as one are relational, and our discipleship means very little until it is lived out in community. Thus, Jesus' teaching cannot be fully absorbed when community is neglected.

The ways we interact with one another display our deepest core values and the condition of our hearts. In our current historical context, with social media "connections" at all-time highs, the ability to connect relationally remains at all-time lows, resulting in the social breakdown evident throughout society. Jesus was the Master Teacher, not only in his ability to connect with the people he taught, but also in the ways he connected them to each other. John recounts Jesus' plea, "Love each other as I have loved you" (John 15:12). He longs for his children to love one another. Jesus' teaching not only instructs us how to practice this, but his life models it. The disciples would learn how to love each other by practicing together, and so do we. It is one thing to read the Bible on my own, which is right

---

[55] Brooks, *How to Know,* 106.

and needed, but in the absence of community, I cannot incorporate the needed transformation.

Pause to Consider:

- Do you agree that spiritual transformation is incomplete when we don't learn in community? If so, why? If not, why not?
- If you are an introvert by nature, how might you incorporate group discussions in ways that can enhance your learning and teaching?

A Word of Caution

While we need each other for spiritual formation, it becomes important to consider ways we help or don't help each other. We rightly should accompany each other on our transformational journeys but must remember that Jesus is whom we follow. David Benner cautions:

> The Christian spiritual journey requires us to overcome the temptation to follow other people rather than Jesus himself. If we are blessed, we will have experiences of seeing him in spiritual friends or other Christians who share our journey. In these circumstances it is sometimes tempting to think that following them is following Jesus. But it is not. Spiritual friends help us most when they make clear that their job is to point the way, not to lead the way. And the Way to which they should point is Jesus.

> An equally important temptation for those seeking to offer spiritual friendship is to assume that one's own route is best for others. How easy it is to think that everyone should meet God in the way and places that I do. How easily I imagine that everyone should follow the same path of prayer, devotion or service as I have followed.
>
> The task of spiritual friends is to help us discern the presence, will and leading of the Spirit of God. Spiritual friends provide a serious disservice when they authoritatively dictate the specific path we should follow. In so doing they seek to give us a map of their own creation. At best, this will distract us from a focus on Jesus and his Spirit. At worst, it leads us to focus on a map rather than God himself—and that is the sin of idolatry.[56]

As we accompany each other on our spiritual journeys, our pilgrimages will contain different trials, paces, roadblocks, traumas, and triumphs that merit consideration and respect. Friends help friends follow Jesus.

Learning in a Cohort

I recently finished my doctoral program within a cohort of about a dozen students/colleagues. I was the oldest in the cohort, and we were a varied group of individuals of different

[56] David G. Benner, *Sacred Companions: The Gift of Spiritual Friendship & Direction* (Downers Grove, IL: InterVarsity Press, 2002), 27–28.

ages, genders, and backgrounds. We commiserated, questioned, shared misunderstandings, encouraged each other as we wrote dissertations, and remained curious about what each other was learning. I think I learned as much from the interactions with my colleagues as I did from any lecture from a professor or individual assignment. I also recently took a year of training for a Christian coaching certification, done with a cohort of thirteen people. I still keep in touch with many of them, as their perspectives greatly enriched the things I learned and experienced.

I fondly remember a community learning experience when I was an eager learner in my early campus ministry days eons ago. The teachings that most stuck with me from then until today, fifty years later, were those done in small groups of students as we discussed different passages of Scripture during our Friday night devotionals. Seldom did one person do all the teaching. We learned from each other. While certainly we need teachers and preachers, we learn from Jesus the value of learning together. From Jesus' example, we can also learn the importance of discussion in a group.

Recently, I have had the opportunity to meet often in a "house church" setting. While "big church" and "small church" all have their strengths and weaknesses, I have felt a deep sense of community, learning, growth, and meaningful fellowship in this small group setting. Interestingly, when we look at early church settings, they varied from place to place without one set model, adapting to meet the needs of the local community.

In my current setting, someone, whomever is hosting the

group that day, presents a biblical thought or study, which then becomes a group discussion. Some of the most profound comments and teachings for me were said by those from whom I least expected to hear them. Not because of their lack of wisdom, but because of their lack of previous opportunity to share. What a wealth of resources becomes available when each person comes with something to give, and is given the opportunity to share it. At other times, we might look at a passage of Scripture from various vantage points, where four groups might look at a teaching of Jesus from four different views according to each person in the story. For example, in Luke 7, it includes the sinful woman, Simon, the other guests, and Jesus. I learned a lot from the other perspectives that people shared. When a church community is large, it seems imperative to enhance teaching through small group settings, where people can learn from each other. Now that we are professional "Zoomers," distance and time constraints can even be overcome, if necessary.

Another way we learn in community is through theological training. Many, if not most denominations require their church leaders to get theological training, knowing the ways teaching can easily veer off course, miss so much, and be misused in all sorts of ways. In my tribe, theological training was viewed negatively for years, thinking it would hinder the practical evangelistic fervor of the church. We paid a price for this, at times teaching as doctrines things made by man. Having recently received theological training, my only regret is that I did not do this earlier, as it has helped me tremendously in my understanding, teaching, and discipleship. It is never too late. I received my doctorate when I was a few months away from turning seventy years old. I am aware that education is a privilege and is not always an option, but many books and online (sometimes free) courses offer opportunities for further education, though they need to be vetted for quality. Seeing this need, I am grateful for many initiatives that have more recently begun in my church stream.[57] My education and training have not decreased my faith and fervor; quite the opposite. I believe it important for ministers and teachers, in order to teach with greater integrity and effectiveness, to receive foundational theological teaching in hermeneutics, surveys of the Old and New Testaments, church history, and what has been called "systematic theology," or basic tenets of subjects such as Christology (the person, nature, and role of Jesus), soteriology (the study of salvation), trinitarian theology (God existing as three persons but one being), pneumatology

[57] Dr. Douglas Jacoby spearheaded the teaching ministries in our church stream decades ago in the UK and then with AIM (Athens Institute of Ministry) and now the International Bible Teaching Ministry, along with others like Gordon Ferguson, who taught Bible in many places around the globe. Tom and Sheila Jones, as publishers and editors, also instituted more education through written resources. In the last decade, schools of missions and teaching ministries have begun in many places around the world. Numerous teaching websites are now available from those who have had theological training. More recently, my church stream has seen the establishment of Mountain Seminary, spearheaded by Dr. Glenn Giles and Dr. Steve Kinnard. Dr. Robert Carrillo provides resources in spiritual formation through thewayministry.global. To further encourage theological training and education, Dr. David Pocta and others have begun a leadership and educational training center, CHORD.

(the study of the Holy Spirit), ecclesiology (the study of the church), and eschatology (the study of death, judgment, and the soul's destiny). While these can sound like heady topics, our understanding of them has great implications for the way we live as Christians. I appreciate a more recent focus on theological education in my church, and I believe that Jesus' example as a learner and teacher should inspire us toward such.

Discerning Together

Another powerful community learning tool I recently discovered has been the practice of community discernment when discussing plans, seeking to determine God's will for a situation. As a group, a discernment session begins by acknowledging the presence of God's Spirit. Then, each person in the room deliberately acknowledges the others in the room as equals. Next, anticipating the group discussion at hand, we intentionally remember those who are not in the room and do not have a seat at the table, considering their unheard voices and needs. Throughout the discussion, prayers are offered along the way, asking the Spirit to give greater clarity. This practice seems in keeping with the teaching and instruction Jesus gave the disciples as they went out, depending on the Spirit's involvement to guide them and following Jesus' example to see and hear people who didn't have "seats at the table." This practice reminds me that without community, we cannot really practice self-sacrifice or love for one another. As mentioned in the previous chapter, Jesus was the master at seeing and hearing people, and we must learn from him how to see and hear each other. Especially those who have different perspectives and backgrounds.

Teaching in Community

Yet another practice meaningful to me as a teacher is community preparation. Whenever I taught in my church group, I would first study and plan my lesson and then send it to a few fellow teachers. Next, in person or online, we would meet to discuss the lesson, which would make the lessons stronger as each person contributed. Whenever I teach or speak to a group, I collaborate with others beforehand. I also do this when I teach through writing, seeking to learn what I may have missed, and how I might have accidentally misrepresented something or said something in a way that lacked clarity or love. I appreciate it when others contribute to my thoughts, as I realize that others have perspectives that I do not, no matter how much I have studied.

While some will not concur with everything I teach or write, I value their input and would not want to proceed without it. I believe it is important to gather views that differ from mine. I continually learn, and there are things that I have taught in the past that I no longer agree with. Though I do not ask for everyone to agree with me nor do I agree with everyone, I deeply appreciate an openness to learn, which I strive to carry. Before I publish a book, I will have requested numerous eyes on it for further input.

There are many times when I find it easier *not* to teach

something I learn and deem as important, but I carry with me my late husband's charge to have the courage to express what I believe to be true. He encouraged me with this shortly before he died, as he knew that some things I was learning and writing about could be challenging for some. I also carry Mark 12:14 in my heart and mind, remembering that Jesus was concerned about the ways of God, not what others thought. Certainly, Jesus' disciples functioned most often in community as they learned from him and each other, and we can learn much from this practice.

Pause to Consider:

- Consider a time when you have learned something important because of being in a group. How did the group process help you learn? In what ways did the group learning process contribute to comradery?
- How might you initiate more ways to practice communal learning and teaching?

Conclusion

As we journey through Jesus' life as the Master Teacher, I pray we let his motivation inspire and empower us to both learn and teach from a heart of love. Jesus' surety of his identity as one coming from God and going to God, and as His beloved Son, can enable us—as we abide in him and he dwells in us—to realize our identity as God's beloved, created in his image.

Jesus, as Master Teacher, reaches to the core of our

foundational beliefs, thus helping us to live out of those. He asks questions, and as we pause to consider these questions, we will often find answers.

Jesus, as Master Teacher, knows and notices us, helping us according to our needs while modeling how to see, hear, and connect with others. The Master Teacher sees us and seeks us, and because of his everlasting love, he longs for relationship with us. Thus, he can be our safest place as we learn to trust him no matter how many people in our lives have proved untrustworthy. As we humbly learn from the Master Teacher, he helps us understand the importance of community for growth. As I began with a prayer, I find no better way to end these pages than with prayer.

Loving Father, Son, and Spirit,
how can we thank you for your mercy that searches for us,
asking where we are and covering our shame?
May your motivation become ours
as we open our eyes to the poor, oppressed, and captives.
Grant us the humility to care,
knowing that you came to redeem us all.
Living Word, let us abide in you
so that the ways we live, learn, and teach
flow out of the love you have put in our hearts.
We can't do this on our own. We need you.
Thank you for becoming flesh and living among us,

giving us your Spirit to stay with us,
comforting us and guiding us into all truth.
How do we thank you for loving us so well that you see and hear us,
giving witness to our lives and
accompanying us on our journeys, even when, especially when,
they are hard, and difficult to understand?
We believe, help our unbelief.
May we live as your beloved,
knowing where we come from and where we are going.
Master Teacher, help us understand the big-picture life lessons
and live by them, knowing your desire to bless us.
May we answer your questions to reveal
the deepest, most vulnerable parts of our heart.
Help us entrust our all to you,
as you love us with tenderness and affection.
Heal us from within
so we can see and hear others, blessing them with your love.
May we trust your timing,
knowing that in our pain you are often closest.
Let your love flow from us to others
so our love for each other is evident
and your kingdom comes on earth as in heaven.
Forgive our lack of faith and trust. Our lack of love.
May we pause to consider your teachings,
prophecies, poetry, questions, and stories

that bring humility, understanding, and wisdom;
to know your steadfast love
and drink it in.
May we receive your words
as one taught from Jesus,
the Master Teacher.
Open our eyes and ears to learn and discern
so that our hearts are filled with you,
bringing others to you,
the Master Teacher

Available at www.ipibooks.com and Amazon.com

Available at
www.ipibooks.com
and
Amazon.com

Available at
www.ipibooks.com
and
Amazon.com

Jeanie Shaw

Every Day Is A New Chance

Available at
www.ipibooks.com
and
Amazon.com

Available at
www.ipibooks.com
and
Amazon.com

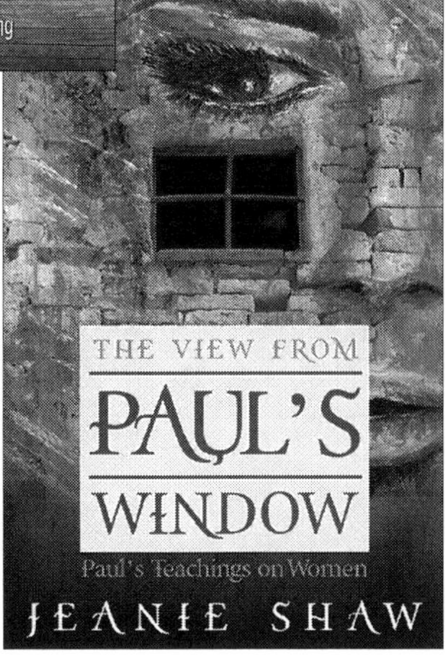

Welcome to the New

SPEAKING OF GOD — DR. JOHN M. OAKES
Spiritual Transformation — Cresenda Jones
MESSIANIC JUDAISM — DOUGLAS JACOBY
Go in the Strength You Have — Rayola Osanya
A HOUSE OF PRAYER — C. SCOTT DAVIS
LOVE, LAUGHTER, AND LAW
Jesus and Mental Health — Marvin K. Lucas
WHAT NOW, GOD? — JEANIE SHAW
SINGLES MINISTRY CAN CHANGE THE WORLD — FERNANDO ALEJANDRO
Mindpowered Singles — CRESENDA JONES
Journey of the SOUL
THE UPWARD CALL — PAT SEMPEL, EDITOR
CALLING OUT THE PEOPLE OF GOD — DOUGLAS JACOBY
PAIN KILLER — R.K. McKEAN
The Sacred Journey
WILDFIRE — DAREN OVERSTREET
The Recovery Journey — TIMOTHY SUMERLIN, PH.D.
This Doesn't Feel Like Love Either — LAMBS

www.ipibooks.com

Made in the USA
Middletown, DE
02 September 2024